A WIDOW'S TOUCH

True Stories of Encouragement & Healing

To Pam: God's blessing you as you journey through the Next chapter of Life. Sheila

Mary M. Hollis

The Next Chapter Widows' Ministry

Honor widows that are widows indeed.

- 1 Timothy 5:3

Library of Congress Control Number: 2016914676
CreateSpace Independent Publishing Platform, North Charleston, SC

Cover design by Jabari Perry

Production Manager & Interior Design by Evertrue Bell

Printed in the United States of America

For special book orders contact: The Next Chapter Widows' Ministry
TNCwidows@gmail.com or www.tncwidows.com

USA $14.99

Dedications

This book is dedicated to my loving husband, Alfornia Hollis. May he rest in peace.

We also dedicate this book to the family members and friends of widows along with the ministers, evangelist and counselors who help widows. We salute you for embracing the wisdom and knowledge from our widows' true stories and recovery strategies.

To Our Contributors

This book is likewise dedicated to the widows who with great humility shared their stories to uplift and encourage others who have become widows. It is our prayer that God will be pleased with the gifts offered by the contributors whose true stories appear in this first volume of *A Widow's Touch*. May these intimate experiences touch your emotions and warm your heart. May they bring you to a better understanding of God's love for us all.

Acknowledgment

I have had the pleasure of working with Mary M. Hollis and several of the other ladies who are a part of The Next Chapter Widows' Ministry for many years. I have been both impressed and inspired by the leadership that exists within the ministry.

As I have said to the members on more than one occasion, we know that none of them voluntarily signed up to be a part of the widow's ministry. But God's grace and mercy can help heal the grieving and wounded hearts through this very effective ministry. This ministry has been, is presently, and will continue to be a blessing to many who may find themselves as widows. Please continue the good work that has begun and be encouraged as you minister and serve both individually and collectively those that God will place in your path.

Also, know that I am one of your biggest supporters and advocates. But even more importantly, remember there is "nothing too hard for God", even as you may find yourselves sometimes in dark and lonely places because of the death of your spouse. Furthermore, we are reminded for those who accepted the Lord as their personal Savior, "to be absent from the body is to be present with the Lord". So, we pray for God's continued comforting presence for all who may read this book, A Widow's Touch, and for any who may experience the passing of your spouse. Please continue to take part in the many social and spiritual events sponsored by The Next Chapter Widows' Ministry. In Service for the Lord.

Rev. Dr. Herman E. Haynes, Jr., Staff Pastor
The Greater Piney Grove Baptist Church – Atlanta, Georgia

Contents

A Widow's Touch

A Widow's Touch

Foreword

A Widow's Touch is a must read. This is by no means "The Next Chapter's" last book. Yes, widows will be blessed by this book, but also the body of Christ and anyone that has an open heart for the hurting. I want to celebrate and applaud all those who have worked with The Next Chapter Widows' Ministry through the years. The essences of this book can be found in the scripture written by Apostle Paul who writes to the young Timothy and instructs him "to honor widows".

For forty years, I have pastored three different churches in Georgia. In all these years, I have witnessed and participated in church budgets and program planning. There are budget line items for everything imaginable: food, food, and more food. But seriously, most churches have no problem allocating church funds and resources for Christian Education, Music, Missions, and Evangelism. However, there has never been a budget or line item for "the widows in need."

A member of our church, who's been a widow for over ten years, sits in our annual meetings where we discuss the church's vision and budget. She would always come to me after the meeting jokingly saying, "Pastor, I am still waiting for the budget committee and leaders to present a plan and budget to care for our widows." We laugh each year and say maybe next year. But it's time to take this ministry command seriously.

Several years ago, a dear friend and Pastor of a nearby church for over thirty years passed after suffering many years with poor health. When my wife and I visited his grieving spouse, she took my hand and looked me in the eye and said, "Bill, I have never even thought of being a widow, now that I am a widow, what am I supposed to do?"

A Widow's Touch

Mary, a loyal and persistent member was thrust into widowhood with her two small children. But God's word is true. He will turn our sorrow and weeping into joy and laughter. Rather than being drown into pity; withdraw from everything or question the will of God, unrealistically Mary embraced her new life and responded indeed as Job did in his loss and emptiness. She turned her test into a testimony. Mary's diligence, persistence and dedication has grown into a movement. THE BEST IS YET TO COME.

Thanks to The Next Chapter Widows' Ministry more widows will receive spiritual coaching and mentoring in an hour and time of challenge and loss.

Dr. William E. Flippin, Sr., Senior Pastor
The Greater Piney Grove Baptist Church — Atlanta, Georgia

Introduction

The Genesis of "The Next Chapter Widows' Ministry"

This book was written to encourage widows and give them comfort while they go through their personal journey of grief. The Next Chapter Widows' Ministry was created by two women after God's own heart. They stepped out on faith with their desire to exemplify love to widows through encouragement and information about the many decisions that widows are confronted within the first three years of losing their spouse.

Sheila A. Coley, President and Mary M. Hollis, Director met through the friendships of their children who attended Greenforest McCalep Christian Academy in Decatur, Georgia. It's truly amazing how God pulls people together to do "His Will". They met and began talking one day on the vision that God gave them about starting the widow's ministry. Sheila is not a widow but they both had a robust resolve and passion to start The Next Chapter Widows' Ministry.

Sheila is an expert financial professional and tax consultant. She's also gifted with organizational and creative skills. In addition to her role as our president she quickly designed our ministry's logo and promotion materials. You name it, she can do it well. It's a blessing to have her in our ministry.

Mary's personal experience of being an accomplished widow alone with her dedication to do "God's Will", contributes to her proficiency in her role as the Director and leader of the emotional aspect of the ministry. As Sheila and Mary continued to talk, God clarified their purpose and He gave them a plan, as of today; together, they have touched hundreds of widows. Together they learned that true human-interest stories touch us in ways we can't always explain, affecting all of us differently. We often gain wisdom from the stories that speaks to our heart. That is what "A Widows' Touch" is all about; speaking to our hearts, encouragement and healing.

A Widow's Touch

What Am I Doing with Widows?

By *Sheila A. Coley*
Stone Mountain, Georgia
President: The Next Chapter Widows' Ministry

Oh God, what am I doing starting a widow's ministry? I'm married! Too soon, Lord! Your sense of humor just isn't funny right now. What widow will talk to me? How will I be received or perceived? How can I be any comfort to them? I had more questions than answers. But I did know that it was God leading me. It certainly wasn't an idea that I would come up with on my own. So, out of obedience, my friend Mary and I started *The Next Chapter Widows' Ministry*!

Women face so many phases of life.

Too often, God sets us on new journeys, very different than the one we had planned or even hoped for. Some days are full of excitement and laughter, while other days are steeped in disappointment, fear and even anger. Women face so many phases of life, from puberty to menopause. I'm reminded of the butterfly that must complete a not-so-easy metamorphosis to reach its full potential and beauty.

A Widow's Touch

Likewise, one day at a time, we must keep going, persevering through the multiple phases of life, even widowhood.

Over the past thirteen years since Mary and I began The Next Chapter, my dad died four months after being diagnosed with liver cancer. My mother was thrust into widowhood after fifty-two years of marriage and was refusing to accept grief. Mom went through a myriad of emotional rollercoaster rides. During it all, I divorced my husband after twenty-one years of marriage.

At this point in my life I have no daddy nor husband.

The men who had loved us and provided for us were gone. Life was different. It's interesting how when they were around, the things that annoyed us and caused arguments became insignificant. The simple things like not having to work, having the cars serviced, lawn manicured, or zipping up the back of the dress was no longer available to us. Sure, the things that annoyed us were gone, but what a price to pay.

Before my divorce, I thought that widows didn't have a choice, so their loss should be more understood.

What I quickly realized was that divorce is the absence of hope which gives the same feeling of no choice. I became fully acquainted with despair, disappointment, shame, anger, fear, denial, and the many characteristics of grief. I had to get it together. Too many days, weeks and months were passing. I had to get okay with looking in the mirror again without seeing a failure, a statistic, and a woman of God who couldn't make her marriage work. Why couldn't God just speak and make it all better? Well, He could. He just didn't (lol)!

A Widow's Touch

Step by step, one hour at a time, before one day at a time. Now, I look back over the last four years that I've been divorced and I am a witness to the promise that God will never leave nor forsake me. God made me do the work to be better and stronger. He assigned angels to me along that journey that kept me safe when I made choices that may not have been bad, but certainly was not best for me. God has shown his loving kindness toward me in my physical, spiritual, mental, emotional and financial life. God is restoring all that has been taken from me. Most miraculously, he is restoring my relationship with my husband by giving us new hearts for each other. How unfair? My mom or other widows don't get a chance to get their husbands back. However, I hope that they will find peace within themselves as they enter the next chapter in their lives.

The Next Chapter taught me about grief.

The Next Chapter has given me an up close and personal perspective on the importance of appreciating your loved one because we never know when the time we have with someone will be the last time. The Next Chapter taught me about grief, which allowed me to be not just supportive of my mom, but understanding of the things she said and did. Grief impacts everyone at some point in life. According to the US Census Bureau, an estimated 700,000 people are widowed each year. That is an enormous number of people that need support on many levels. I am spiritually and professionally devoted to financial wellness in families to prevent minimal to catastrophic losses when a loved one passes, especially the breadwinner.

A Widow's Touch

What bride wants a "widow's readiness kit?"

However, too often, we refuse to have the conversation that must be had. We must insist on preventing legal and financial ruins due to poor planning or lack of planning. Husbands and wives who spend years building a legacy of tangibles and intangibles must take the time to protect their precious possessions. I have experienced both deep wounds and deep healing. Now, it's time for me to help as many others as my time left here will allow.

I envision water walking widows.

I learned from my Bible Study Fellowship that no matter what the loss may be, God will not allow any of our suffering to be wasted. Allow God to take that pain and make it the foundation to build your destiny. I envision water walking widows. These are women who have been summoned by God to walk through the valley of the shadow of death called widowhood, but came through as pure gold. These awesome women of God would have developed insurmountable power through conquering more than they ever thought they could. These widows will not be frazzled by the term widow, but use it as a VIP card that carries rights commanded by God, "to honor widows that are widows in deed".

Just watch what incredible and awesome plans God has for you, just because...He loves you! The Next Chapter Widow's Ministry is more than a visit, a call, a card! We simply touch widows with personal prayers of comfort, verbal exchange and a variety of individual and group fellowship events. We laugh and cry together and enjoy our amazing sisterhood.

For I know the plans I have for you, declares the Lord. -Jeremiah 29:11

A Widow's Touch

God Prepared Me for the Storm

By Mary M. Hollis
Decatur, Georgia
Director: The Next Chapter Widows' Ministry

As of today, I have watched 9,125 days go by where the sun has risen and on those same days the sun has softly set. I have been a widow for twenty-five years and I am not just living I am thriving. My life is not just good, it's great. It's all because God prepared me for the storm that came when my husband Alfornia (AL) Hollis died leaving me with a four-year old daughter and ten-month old son. I didn't understand God's plan at the time, he took my best friend. However, looking back over the many years and days, I can clearly see that God put a strategic plan in Al's head and heart as he started his life as a husband and father.

I know it had to be God.

Al was a good husband, father, lover, friend and good neighbor. His dedication to his family was obvious to everyone. In Al's own way he made sure that we were going to be alright in his absence. I know it had to be God because Al and I did not discuss the many things he did to prepare for the storm. For example; Al significantly increased the life insurance policy we

7

had on him. He loved making our lawn the most beautiful on our block. He found time to work part time jobs; while working full-time as a firefighter. He zealously built up his social security earnings for us all, without saying a word to me.

Al loved shopping at big box stores, like Walmart and Home Depot. He often purchased household items in bulk. It was months after his passing before I had to go shopping. The first Christmas and six months after Al died, I went into his clothes closet to begin gathering things to give away. I found a bag of brand new toys he had bought for our kids. Instantly I was taken away. All I could do was sit there alone and cry wishing he was still here. I saw his obedience to God's voice as he did so many warm things for us prior to his departure.

I thought I was going to have a nervous breakdown.

Another reason my life is better than good, is that God prepared me several years before I met Al for the storm, as well. I was going through a tough emotional time that was driven by a heart-breaking experience. I thought I was going to have a nervous breakdown. But God kept me, yes, he kept me from falling apart. God sent a special angel to me that read books with me, that encouraged and motivated me to move on.

My assigned angel helped me inhale certain scriptures whenever I felt I was weak and the enemy tried to attack my mind. Scriptures like "Be still and know I am God"; Psalm 23, 27, 37 and 91. These scriptures were my protection from the enemy to keep me from losing my mind. It was a long journey getting through the storm's challenges but I made it, thanks to the village of people God sent to me and the kids. My family received words of encouragement from so many people. My neighbors cut our grass for two months. My girlfriends from New York, Atlanta and surrounding areas were all there for me. I never realized how many caring, faithful and loyal friends I had; until the storm hit. Church members never skipped a beat sharing words of wisdom every weekend. Most of all, God continued to let me know that He was there and He would never leave nor forsake me. Even with my strong belief, I still questioned God about how I was going to pay the mortgage and keep the lights on.

Two weeks after my husband's death, I went to pick up his last paycheck. In true astonishment, there laid a seven-thousand-dollar check. The check was a combination of his last two work weeks and his unused worked days. Al never took a day off from work, for any reason. This was not only a sign and answer from God; it was another one of Al's merciful ways of caring for his family. Twenty-five years later; God continues to walk this journey with me and my children. He continued to answer my questions and he gave me proof along the way.

Deuteronomy 31:8 (NIV) says, "The Lord himself goes before you and will be with you; He will never leave you nor forsake you." As I continued to go through this journey of grief and raising my children, God sent friends, families, neighbors and church members to help me and my children.

I can't leave out the coaches, and the barber who was a great mentor for my son. It was a real village that God sent to rescue me and supply me with all that I lacked while moving through the storm.

On a bright Sunday morning, the storm "knocked" on my door.

A Widow's Touch

At 7:30 a.m. there was a loud knock at the door. My life changed that morning, my husband for six years had a massive heart attack at work. Al, was a great firefighter for twenty-four and a half years. Standing at my front door was several firemen from Al's fire station. I knew something was wrong.

The firemen had a look on their faces; that when you see it you know the news is not good. The words: "Mrs. Hollis; we have sad news", that made my heart stop beating. My eyes welded up and when I heard the fireman say "Al has been taken to the hospital, he had a heart attack".

I struggled to get dressed and to get my kids out of bed and dressed. Finally, one of the fireman, said. "Can you call someone that can help you with your children?" I called my girlfriend Geri, within minutes she arrived. She calmed me down, helped me get dressed and told me to go see about Al. Geri pushed me out of the door and assured me that my children would be fine.

During all of this; I was thinking that Al was OK!

As I walked to the hospital entrance, my heart started pounding. It seemed like every fireman from the nearby stations were there, for Al. They cleared a path as I entered the hospital. I knew then, that Al was gone. My first thought was; why would my God let this happen to a great man like Al? Yes, I questioned God, I needed answers, right then. However, God showed me over the first six months after we buried Al; why he was called home.

Later, I realized, I was asking God questions after the storm had hit, questions like; "Why did my husband die?" "Why was I left to raise two young babies by myself?" God chose to answer every question after the storm settled and when he knew; I was ready to hear and take in his good will.

Shortly after, Al's passing; I found myself frequently meeting widows. It was amazing; through my job, neighborhood, friends of friends and my church; women would be in conversation and say "I am a widow" and I would respond, "so am I".

Once again, I asked my God, why do I keep bumping into all of these widows? His answer, came to me as clear as the morning sun. I heard him whispering in my ear—not once, but several times. "Mary, you had to become a widow to effectively encourage other widows."

God has given me peace. I moved through these thoughts, I felt a special widow's touch. Now, I feel protected and safe as I watch my children and grandchildren live a Godly life. He has supplied us with our needs. Yes, there were rough times and the roads have not always been straight but He has given me the strength and the courage to persevere. I love my Heavenly Father so much and I am happy that I know Him, even while I am still learning more about Him at this time in my life. Yes, I received the answers I was seeking and I have accepted my calling to support widowed women for thirteen years now. We clearly defined our purpose to encourage widows as they are going through the grieving process.

Launching our ministry.

Sheila and I launched our ministry, and I am now a proud and eager Director and Biblical Counselor for widowed woman. I gracefully accepted many banking jobs throughout my career.

However, my widow's ministry by-far is more rewarding than all that I have done throughout my work life.

Today as I transcribe this book, my daughter, Alexcia, is thirty and married to Johnnie my wonderful son-in-law. I now have two precious grandchildren, Josiah and Journee. Alexcia earned her Bachelor's Degree in Journalism and her Master's Degree in Early Childhood Education from Georgia State University. What a blessing to see her grow into a successful and highly motivated teacher.

My son, Allan, is twenty-six, now. He graduated from Georgia State University, as well; with a Computer Science Degree. For the last two years, he's been employed as a Software Developer in Atlanta. Even though my life as a widow was full of challenges, God has blessed me with two beautiful and successful children.

The following courses prepared me for the role as Director of The Next Chapter Widows' Ministry. I have a certification in Biblical Counseling in titled "Caring for People God's Way" through the American Association of Christian Counselors from Light University located in Forest, Virginia. In addition, I am a certified leader and facilitator of the Worldwide Discipleship Association's curriculum "Restoring Your Heart" at The Greater Piney Grove Baptist Church in Atlanta, Georgia.

My Heavenly Father, has been a father to the fatherless. I thank God every day for helping me understand how to survive and move through the storm. Sometime you must lose to win, in the game of life. Be strong in the Lord, stand on his words, and be encouraged. He will never leave you nor forsake you. To God Be the Glory.

A Widow's Touch

I will always remember these two scriptures: "And we know that all things work together for good to them that love God, to them who are called according to his purpose." Romans 8:28

"Be strong and courageous. Do not be afraid: Do not be discouraged, for the Lord your God will be with you wherever you go." --Joshua 1:9 (NIV)

Finally, after working forty-years in the banking industry, I have completely transitioned out of the corporate world into a lifelong commitment to work fulltime doing "God's Will": encouraging, supporting, helping and healing widows.

Recovering from Your Loss is Possible!

To: The Women in Our Widows' Ministry,

Your world may have been shattered when your husband, the one you loved so dearly, transitioned. Feel comforted in knowing that it is possible to gain joy again. You can recover from your loss. Every challenge brings a new opportunity for you to rebalance your life. You can expect good to come out of every situation. Our desire is that this book provides support and encouragement as you move through grief to healing. Enclosed are true, and sincere examples of how difficult times *do not* have to be handled alone.

Sincerely,

Sheila A. Coley, President & Mary M. Hollis, Director
The Next Chapter Widows' Ministry

A Widow's First Six Months

We prayed to God for inspiration on how to motivate the members of *"The Next Chapter Widows' Ministry"* on how to share their stories. We were hearing incredible stories that we knew would help other widows if only they could hear or read about what others have gone through. As we pondered over ways to encourage other widows to forge ahead and to not feel forsaken. We decided to ask questions and to capture the responses as they are formatted in this book. Our questions led to more questions. The stories led to healing, encouragement and empowerment.

However, we gave God the "Glory", as we prayed for a process to share the many gifts of stories, lessons and experiences we received. He instantly responded with a long list of personal questions that only He could know, because the widows went directly to Him with these questions and concerns in the first six months of their loss.

The questions that God gave us, served as thought-starters for many of our widows. It allowed them to reflect on their feelings, to pull from their memory some of the most intricate experiences that they had when they lose the most important person in their lives. The inserts in this book are here because of the courage and the strong desire of *"The Next Chapters Widows' Ministry"* to help widows.

We pray that you find a comfortable spot or zone that will provide the strength that you need and the power to forge ahead with your life. As we, make every effort to connect with our widows in ways that helps them to feel comfortable when sharing their experiences. As you read their responses and stories we pray that you find strength in God and consider joining "The Next Chapter Widows' Ministry" so you can become a part of our next chapters.

A Widow's Touch

Lord, God, Why?

By Bennie Franklin
Decatur, Georgia

"Lord, where do we go from here?"

"Lord, will you dry up my tears so I can go out among people without crying?"

"Lord, why do I find myself in this place, without Curtis?"

A Widow's Touch

Taking His Clothes Out of the Closet

Bernice Scott

Decatur, Georgia

Every day for three to four weeks, I went into James' closet and touched, hugged and smelled his clothes. Of course, I cried through this process, but I continued. One morning, I woke up and decided to clean out my husband's closet. I gave some of his clothes and shoes to my neighbor, some clothes to my church ministry and the other things to Goodwill. I knew it was the thing to do. I believe that James and God were pleased.

A Widow's Touch

He Was Comical and Loved to Tell Jokes

By Dwendyl Suggs
Atlanta, Georgia

"What do you miss most about Alvin?"

My husband, was very comical and he loved to make jokes. Every day around 5:00 pm, Al would call me to see if I had left work and to ask about dinner? He would ask "Are you cooking?" "Am I cooking?" "Do you want to go out to eat?" I never thought about it until my first week back at work. On my way home, I found myself waiting for the phone call that will never happen again. When the weather was bad in the mornings on the way to work, Al would call to see if I made it or just call to say something quick. I knew that was his way to make him feel at ease that I was safely at work.

Al's smile kept us connected.

He would smile when I walked in the door from work or when I had not seen him in a couple of hours. It was such a flirtatious way he had. He gave me such a sense of security that I cannot explain but it made me feel so safe, wanted and loved. Many times, when events happen whether it was a news event, something in the city or a family concern. I often missed what he would have said on the subject. Al was known to have an opinion on every topic and while I did not agree with some of his thoughts, I missed hearing his take on the matter. My daughters and I always said "Wonder what Al would have said or done if he was here?"

I recently had to make some major financial decisions alone. This was very difficult because Al and I made all our monetary decisions together. We would weigh out the pros and cons, advantages and disadvantages but we always agreed on the next steps. I missed his wisdom and his way of thinking through things. I yearned to have the security of knowing that we were in our marriage together, again.

As I am writing these comments, it just hit me that I missed Al but I have the security of GOD. I have not missed a beat, with as small as what is for dinner, a smile or as large as major decisions that will affect my future. It has been tough but sometimes I think Al is still here supporting my every thought.

"What has been your most difficult moments?"

Al was into old school music from the 70's and 80's and I knew all his favorites tunes. Early on he recorded his favorite songs onto audio tapes because he said "music today isn't as good as old music was, back in the day".

Later, he spent hours transferring his music again to CDs. Traveling to visit my mom is a five-hour drive which is also on a route that had very low radio signals. As we travel through the small towns—it was a perfect time for Al to play his CD collection. Sometimes I can hear him singing in my ears as he did when we used to take those road trips.

It still brings tears to my eyes.

A Widow's Touch

I believe that those trips were some of Al's happiest moments. He loved, James Brown's music and the day after his passing I had to go on an errand and one of Mr. Brown's songs came on the radio. A part of me wanted to melt and a part of me said, that was God's way of saying AL is with me and he is just fine.

We would drive to New York every summer when the girls were young and talk about the trip for weeks getting food, planning stops and our conversations there and back stayed amazingly special—just the four of us were in a world of our own. It's quite different now, Al is gone and the girls are grown. Today there's different conversations, different ways of traveling and different places to go; I do miss the simple things that were so awesome to me. Things like family gatherings especially with Al's family. They all remind me that he's not here to enjoy or share in the noise, excitement, decisions and planning of these events. He always had an opinion and he was usually funny. He brought so much laughter into our lives.

In thinking of the future, it is difficult for me to contemplate he would not be here when the girls decide to get married and have children. We talked about what we would do when we have a grandchild—he would have been the best granddad. Difficult moments like this make me miss him and wonder "the ifs".

Prior to moving out of the house that Al and I had for twenty-three years, I would visualize him sitting in his favorite recliner chair. I could see him placing his keys on the kitchen counter. Seeing him in bed looking at TV or reading his emails on the computer in the den are two of my favorite memories. For two years, I thought I had lost my mind or I was experiencing some bad dreams—I wanted to wake up to see just what was going on. These dreams and visions are not as difficult anymore because I made the decision to move to a much smaller place in another part of the city. Now I wonder how he would have liked this place—sometimes it never stops. However, it does get easier—thanks to God's help and lots of prayers.

A Widow's Touch

I Know God's Power

By Shirley McPherson
Decatur, Georgia

Twice in my life, I experienced God's true power. Bobby and I tried for years to birth a child. We gave up and decided that God had other plans for us.

The Gift of Life.

God's master plan was for me to not be alone. Twelve-years after our marriage; He gave us a beautiful daughter. We named her Summer. We often referred to her as our miracle baby. A better nickname for Summer is "angel". She's one of those millennials, now twenty-one who genuinely cares for the elder generation. She's not afraid to express appreciation and kindness for the aging. A brief example of how Summer, stands out in the crowd. When a sister widow, Martha Jefferson passed; I couldn't attend her funeral. Summer, decided on her own, that she would go to represent me. She knew how badly I wanted to attend. Summer graduated from undergraduate school in December 2015 and is now working on her law degree. Bobby and I together, enjoyed seventeen years with our beloved miracle baby. Now, I have her all to myself.

A Widow's Touch

After thirty-years of marriage, I lost Bobby in 2013. Before that time, I had prayed using many scriptures saying to God I will trust you through it all. You are God and you know all things; you are the comforter; you are the almighty God. Each day I felt God's peace throughout my journey.

Some of these days and special occasions, I was sad and lonely, but at the end of the day I normally felt better. I knew God was in control and he is the author and finisher of my faith. I continue to hold on to the promises that He said in his words.

Lift your head and keep looking up.

My husband's spirit is with me and I can hear him saying things like "lift your head and keep looking up". I tried after Bobby died to be strong in God. I knew of God's power and have seen so many miracles like the gift of my daughter, Summer. I knew without a doubt, God would see me through.

At first, I became busy and then months later, a spiritual awaking came over me to let me know God was still guiding me through the process. I felt the presence of Him speaking to me every step of the way. It gave me strength like He promised He would.

A Widow's Touch

Sleeping Alone After the Death of My Husband

By Vera McKenzie
Decatur, Georgia

Sleeping alone after the sudden death of my husband was very traumatic. I couldn't bring myself to go to bed so I stayed up as late as I could. Once in bed I found myself staying on the side of the bed that I claimed as mine very early in our marriage. I was afraid to move because I knew that the other side of the bed was missing Eli, my husband of almost thirty-five years. I would also wake up thinking that my husband was in the bed with me only to realize I was dreaming.

Many nights I lay in bed and the tears would just roll down my face because of the pain of my loss. I missed the pillow talk, Eli's warm body next to mine and the intimacy. I continue to wake up in the middle of the night wishing that he was here with me. The loneliness is agonizing. I have come to accept that it was God's will that my husband was called home to be with the Lord and that God does not make any mistakes. The pain persists but I continue to trust and believe in God.

A Widow's Touch

I Felt His Spirit in the Room

By Ollie Penn
Lithonia, Georgia

"What feelings did you experience sleeping alone at night?"

Sometimes, I just didn't want to be alone, especially at night. I missed him so much. Sometimes I felt so bad at night, not having Floyd close to me. I asked God, can you please let him physically visit me for a while? Shortly after my prayer, I felt God's spirit in the room and I could feel Floyd's warmth surrounding me. I thank God for the visit for I know Floyd is home with Him.

A Widow's Touch

My Protector is Gone!

By Florence Bonaparte
Walterboro, South Carolina

"What were some of the feelings and doubt you felt when Mack died?"

We were married for fifty-three wonderful years. When Mack died, I felt like a zombie. I couldn't believe he was gone. I have had many relatives to pass away but losing a spouse was harder than any other member of the family: mother, father, sister, brother, children or grandparents. During this time, I was just going through the motion. I dreamt about Mack every night for two years straight. Mack was a kind and giving person. He was quiet and reserved but very observant of things happening around us. He was my protector.

After he passed, I thought often about how great it would have been if we had spent more quality time together. When we saved money for a honeymoon or vacation, we would spend it helping other family members or becoming pregnant or other emergencies. So, we put it off again and again.

The most important suggestion I want to give to other couples, please spend quality time with each other.

A Widow's Touch

The Fire, Death and Rebuilding Our Home

By Martha Jefferson (Deceased 11/15/2015)
Atlanta, Georgia

"Martha, your husband's death, the fire, and living in your house later. Tell me about your journey through your grief process?"

On February 9, 2011, a house fire turned my world upside down. My world changed in a blink of an eye. Lamar my husband, survived the fire. However, due to excessive smoke inhalation and health complications he passed away on June 11, 2011. Of course, this was a difficult time but my faith truly helped me stay uplifted. Lamar and I had a love affair that radiated love daily.

Holding on to God's unchanging hands has truly been a testimony in my life. Life itself is truly a journey. Although, it seemed like a hard task initially, with prayer and time I decided to rebuild my home. As I transitioned back into the house, each day became easier. It was definitely a sense of peace in the home. For over thirty-five years, the home held memories of warm smiles, hugs and kisses. Our goal for our home was to leave a legacy behind for generations to come.

A Widow's Touch

God truly gives us strength to get through each day. As I continued my widow's journey, I was reminded of two of my most favorite bible verses:

"Cast all your cares on him for he cares for you". 1 Peter 5:7

"I can do all things through Christ who strengthens me." Philippians 4:13

Always remember to keep Him first in your life and be blessed.

A Widow's Touch

Fifty-Plus Years of Protection

By "Momma" Ocie E. Davis
Brunswick, Georgia

"Ocie, you were married to your husband for fifty-two years. What was the hardest experience you dealt with during the first three years after he passed?"

My hardest experience as a widow was losing my husband Pastor George E. Davis, Sr.; the next hardship was having to make decisions without George. I'm talking about the big decisions concerning finances, house and car maintenance, and handling my own personal health issues were extremely challenging. But, even the little decisions like what to eat, whether to attend certain events, and interacting with family and friends would often be traumatic.

My husband did everything for me! I had to learn to take care of myself and trust others to advise me. I couldn't have done it without my children and special people like Mary Hollis, who would call and check on me. When I was told that he had stage four liver cancer and only a short time to live, I asked God to give us more time. George died four months later.

Now, making decisions are still difficult. However, I am ten years stronger and I've learned to depend on God for everything.

A Widow's Touch

This Can't Be Love

By Tracy Lowe
Covington, Georgia

As a young girl, I didn't have the dreams some girls had of a big wedding, a beautiful dress, and a large reception. As I grew up I was in one bad relationship after another and I had counted myself out of the possibilities of marriage. Enduring both physical and mental abuse from men was a major portion of my life and the crazy thing was I knew better. I grew up in a home where my father and mother loved each other, very rarely would I see them fight or fuss.

The teacher instinct, in me.

I found myself with men I wanted to save and help, that was the teacher instinct in me. I was that loving and caring nurturer. I suffered so much at the hands of men I thought loved me. Often, I would look into the mirror and say; "Who would want to marry me?" My self-esteem was so low from dealing with men who were broken and who ended up breaking me. Then one day I met this man while at a party, he was so confident and so sure of himself. I was talking to one of my male friends when he approached me. I thought he was very cute so I instantly began to blush; but I was also a little

39

taken back because of all the bad relationships I had encountered. We exchanged numbers and the rest was history. Tony was the peanut butter to my jelly, he was the love of my life. I knew that, even though I never had dreams of marriage and I had nearly counted it out of my life.

Tony made me rethink it all!!!

He was so funny so sociable and my parents loved him. Like any other couple, we had ups and downs, our relationship was so far from perfect. He never belittled me or tried to hurt me on purpose. I loved that man!

We would go out of town often and we frequently went to the Falcons games and we would always have a great time. But there was a part of me that questioned would anything other than dating happen for us. We had been together for almost five years and we had never discussed it. One day I began to feel strange and I knew something was wrong with me, but I was in denial. I couldn't keep anything down, I couldn't sleep, and I felt bad. So, I decided to go and get a pregnancy test. I did and I was pregnant and scared.

I wasn't married and living in my parents' home and now pregnant. I didn't know how Tony would react to our big news. Well, when I told him he was excited and then came the big question. "When are we getting married???" I was literally knocked off my feet. The "question" I never thought I would hear. The "question" I felt I wasn't worthy of hearing but here was this man that I loved that treated me the way my father treated my mother asking me to marry him, Yeah!

Then my low self-esteem kicked in. I thought, why was he asking me this? Was it just because I was pregnant? So, I asked him, why are you asking me to marry you? His exact words were "we are now a complete family and I love you and my folks love you, too. I wanted to ask you before this but I didn't have the nerve; this news gave me all the courage I needed". At that moment, I knew he loved me and this was as real as it can get!

Here comes the bride.

Well, we decided on a very simple marriage ceremony. We had just closed on our new home and baby Clarkston was on the way! As we sat waiting to be married at the courthouse; I was nervous as can be, because we were getting married on the date his parents married, who were no longer together. I would periodically look around the room while he cracked jokes and all I could do is sweat and nibble on my nails. I began to pray and ask God to give me strength and instantly God gave it to me.

I looked around at all the smiling faces of the people close to us. Tony's grandparents were there and they don't normally leave Macon, Georgia for anything, at that moment, I knew without a doubt that I was truly blessed!!

The "knock" on the door that I will never forget.

Well, Clarkston's now eight months old and its Daddy's birthday. I cooked a big dinner and bought us hats to wear to surprise Tony when he got home from work. He was so surprised; the smile on his face was priceless. A few weeks later I had just put Clarkston down for a nap when I heard a knock at the door. It was weird because we don't get company like that. I knew it wasn't Tony because he had called about an hour earlier and said he was on his way home, after stopping by his mothers to feed her dogs. I looked out the peep hole and it was Newton County's Sherriff Department. I knew at that very moment something wasn't right. As the Sherriff began to talk; I began to go deaf in both ears not wanting to hear what he was saying. I was reading his lips; "Your husband has been in a car accident." I began to scream and told him I didn't want to hear any more, I ran for my daughter who was still asleep. As I grabbed her, I instantly begin to call on the Lord asking, Why? What have I done to deserve this? My life was just coming together and now this.

Put on your Big Girl Panties

I had so many moments of feeling alone and that no one understood what I was experiencing. I would be praising God one moment and questioning him the next. One day I was in the store and this lady randomly begin to talk to me, this happened often. In that conversation, I began to tell her my story and she said to me.

"Baby, whenever you feel low and down go inside your prayer closet and cry till you can't cry anymore. When you are done and ready to come out with a smile on your face and a prayer in your heart then and only then, ask God to help you through the pain."

That's what I did, time and time again and life began to feel better. I knew that I had to get better not only for myself but for my daughter. I knew that my story was going to help someone else, someday. My mother told me that everything that happens to us isn't always about us personally. It's God's way of using us to help someone else get through. I held on to these very words and since then I have told my story, I'm sure over a hundred times. Gaining more courage allowed me to finish school and get my Bachelor's Degree in Communication. Soon I will complete the work I am doing to earn my Master's in Early Childhood Education. I found time to participate as my daughter's Girl Scout Troop Leader and the PTO President at my daughter's school. While on this widow's path, I've been helped by a lot of great people who have the resources to help me.

Joining The Next Chapter Widows' Ministry helped me to see that I was not in this alone. Watching other ladies with similar stories share their pain and how they pressed on, was, exactly what I needed. I truly can't explain it, but I know that it may not be the life I asked God for but it was the life God choose for me because he knew I was the woman for the job!

A Widow's Touch

Reflections with Answered Questions

By Ann Morris, (Deceased 12/22/2015 at age 94)
Decatur, Georgia

Hello, how are you? Now that I have your attention, I'd like to share with you an article that impressed me. I received this at a recent retreat. It is titled *"Realization"* and no author was given; therefore, she is unknown to me. I'm using it to introduce my journey into the next chapter of my life as a widow.

Who Am I? *I'm an African American Woman!*

What makes me strong? *My heritage!*

What makes me weak? *My fears!*

What make me whole? *My God!*

What keeps me standing? *My Faith!*

What makes me compassionate? *My selflessness!*

What makes me honest? *My integrity!*

What sustains my mind? *My quest for knowledge!*

A Widow's Touch

What teaches me all lessons? My mistakes!

What lifts my head high? My pride!

What if I can't go on? Not an option!

What makes me victorious? My courage to climb!

What makes me competent? My confidence!

What makes me sensual? My insatiable essence!

What makes me beautiful? My everything!

What makes me a woman? My heart!

Who say I need love? I do!

What empowers me? Me!

Who am I? I am an African American WOMAN!

After reading "Realization", I became aware that much information is obtained using the question and answer approach, so I've chosen to follow the same format for my venture into "The Next Chapter Widows' Ministry". It may not be appropriate, sensible, clear or enough information. None the less, here it goes.

Who are you? I am proud to be an African American woman, who is widowed and ninety-one years old. I am independent, the mother of one son and "Mom-Mom" to six grandchildren, six great-grandchildren an anticipating the birth of two more great-grandchildren, soon.

How were you able to adjust to being widowed?

A Widow's Touch

I was blessed and fortunate to have the realization that it had become "me" instead of "we" and the loss was one that I must accept and adjust to. It was easier for me than with some who are left alone, since my husband John was traveling a good bit, he was employed by the Merchant Marines after fulfilling his military service in the Navy.

How did you cope with the loss of your husband?

Shortly after my dear husband John passed, my attention was diverted from grieving for someone I loved dearly, to caring for my two granddaughters, Janelle four, and Anessa two. They filled the void of me being lonely and missing my husband of thirty-two years.

How do you respond to your ideals, spiritual life and general philosophy?

I am proud, pleased and happy to know my Heavenly Father is my protector and the guiding force in my life. So, I don't have to worry. I believe that when I continually act and do things that are favorable to my Lord and Savior, my blessings will be well and continuous.

Do you have financial worries?

Not really, I know my income and my limitations so I give serious thought when spending. I realize that my wants and needs are different as I grow older. I've learned how to sensibly look at my clothes and recycle often or I use some things that I had almost forgotten. I am frequently complimented on my sense of style.

What about your social life and down time? How have you dealt with that?

Basically, I think the answer is to keep busy. It helps to focus on what I am doing or need to do rather than what I am unable to do. I have found it rewarding to bake and decorate special occasion cakes, join sorority activities, play solitaire, play scrabble and talk on the phone. My card group "Pinochle Sistahs" meets every other week, and I look forward to the fellowship and the opportunity to host them. And I now recognize that the computer fills a great void and is a 'pretty good companion'.

I have also found rewarding satisfaction in my church attending and participating in some of its many programs. I've traveled twice as a missionary to Haiti and to Jamaica. I've served ten years as President of our church's Senior group called "Keenagers": and it has been enjoyable and it's kept me busy.

If you were to make a one sentence statement that serves as your path to follow or guiding light in your life, what would it be?

I would say "The Golden Rule; Do unto others as you would have them do unto you".

A Widow's Touch

Love in Black and White

By Venesa Wingo-Wright
Stone Mountain, Georgia

"Hey baby, are you a nurse?"

I looked at this white boy and told him I was the dance teacher and not a nurse, that's how it all began.

I was a black girl from New Jersey just out of college who moved to Atlanta because a friend told me about the inexpensive apartments there. I had a job and only by the grace of God was I able to transfer to the Atlanta office. I attended a majority white high school and college; where I studied dance and preschool education. Robert was a good looking white guy. He was a big guy with a gentle soul who grew up in East Atlanta and graduated from a majority black high school. He was a semi-pro football player, a basketball and baseball coach and no matter where he went people knew him. I remember when we went to Disney World and someone yelled out; "hello Wingo". We were a pair, opposites, yet the same.

Robert was a basketball coach at the recreation center where I was teaching dance. He asked me out the first day I started to work at the recreation center and several times after that; but I kept turning him down. After several days of him not asking me out. I went to the gym where he was bouncing a basketball and I said, "Hi". He didn't even look at me and he kept bouncing that ball. I asked; "What are you doing (as if I couldn't see what he was doing)?" I thought, how dare you ignore me and how dare you not ask me out again? So, I said to him, "I'd like to go out with you." He looked at me with those soft brown and green eyes and with a big smirk on his face and said; "I'd love to go out with you, too". That was the beginning of a love story that lasted through twenty-seven years of love, marriage, birth of our son RJ, a miscarriage of our daughter Candace, and birth of our granddaughter Dana and the final kiss I gave him before he walked into our bedroom and died.

Blah! Blah! Blah

Everyone kept telling me "you are so strong". "You know God does not make a mistake". Really, I'm thinking, well he just made his first mistake (forgive me Lord). Now the bereavement committee is at my house telling me the steps to bury my husband and all I can hear is blah, blah, blah.

I was introduced to The Next Chapter Widows' Ministry almost two weeks after my husband Robert had died. My friend and fellow choir member, Brenda, indicated that they were going to have a Valentine Day lunch at a restaurant for the widows. At first, I was hesitant because I didn't know anyone attending but Brenda. I went and everyone especially Mary and Sheila, the founders of the ministry, welcomed me with open arms. We were serenaded by a nice man, given a flower, and gift bag. They gave advice about what a widow should do and we were given helpful resources and information. It was a blessing that I attended this event because I was sad and depressed about Robert's passing and having to spend Valentine's Day without my soul mate for the first time was heart breaking.

The Next Chapter Widows' Ministry came to my rescue; I have been a member ever since. I enjoy the monthly meetings and outing as well as other fun things we do. We were at a restaurant and we were having a great time laughing and enjoying each other. A lady from a nearby table asked; "what kind of group are you?" I responded that we are a widow's ministry. They were surprised to hear and see widows having fun again.

Frozen

My journey continues. I was in Wal-Mart buying some food for Thanksgiving. This was going to be the first Thanksgiving without my husband. It was going to be just my son and me and I took a chance and went there just like Robert and I use to do. I was pushing the cart when I started having this feeling down in my stomach. It felt like an ocean wave that was slowly heading onto the shore and getting bigger and bigger along the way. I thought I was going to throw up. I started getting hot and felt like I couldn't breathe. As I looked around, I was getting depressed because everyone was happy getting stuff for Thanksgiving and I'm drowning in sorrow. As I walked faster and faster I stopped suddenly and lean over the cart. I was panicking, I stopped and I was frozen right there in the middle of the main isle of the store. I began crying, sobbing, and boohooing out loud with tears streaming down my face, trembling saying, 'Oh God, Oooh Robert'.

A Widow's Touch

People stopped and tried to help me but I couldn't take another step. I needed help and I called another widow, Brenda my friend, who has been supporting me and reassuring me since my Robert died, that I was not crazy uttering my feelings. She's had those feeling also after her husband passed away.

She answered the phone and asked where I was; I told her Wal-Mart and she asked; "which one?" I told her and by the grace of God she was at the same Wal-Mart, in the parking lot about to leave. When she finally came rushing in I almost collapsed in her arms. Brenda; to the rescue! She comforted me and reminded me, God has it all under control and the ocean wave I felt went away.

Me too.

I have a picture of my husband and his obituary in my bible. I was listening to the newest member of our widow's ministry tell us her story and I said; "me too". This was my latest "me too" experience I've had with this ministry. I found out that I am not the only one who keeps their husband's belongings, sleep in his shirts, visit his grave and tell him what happened that day, spray his cologne on his clothes and stand there sniffing; it's like a hound dog. I kissed his picture so much its fading. I even transferred his voice from one of the videos of him to my cell phone so I can hear his voice wherever I am. The list goes on and on. I finally get it; God is in control and he will never leave me nor forsake me and that was reassuring to know. So, I began to trust God in his words.

I'm mad because my husband died and left me!

He is supposed to be here loving and protecting me. I want my husband to caress my breasts and kiss me all over again. I wanted him to drive me around at night and when I had to drive out of the state. He knows I can't see very well at night.

Another chance for happiness.

Entering the next chapter of my life allowed me to love again. God blessed me with another wonderful man named Johnnie who was an old "beau" forty-years ago, we got married December 2015 and I couldn't be happier. I never thought I would have another man in my life that I could trust and who would love, protect and care for me. All the things I questioned God about after Robert died have been answered. Thank you, God, and I am ready for the next chapter of my life.

A Widow's Touch

I Couldn't Face the Real World

By Mandy Walker
Decatur, Georgia

I am a native of Yazoo City, Mississippi where I married Reverend David Walker. We relocated to Los Angeles, California for approximately twenty-five years before moving to Georgia in 1994. We were parents of one daughter (Nichelle) and son (David Jr.) and grandparents of six, one granddaughter (Tiara) and five grandsons (Darnell, Kyre, Dennis Jr., Damian and Damare).

David and I were married for almost forty years before God called him home. It was January 2004 when my husband's health began to fail. He was diagnosed with pancreatic cancer and only had a few months left for us to be together. On May 11, 2004, God called him home. We had a great marriage and I miss him. It was hard to explain how I felt. My heart hurt so bad I felt I couldn't live without my husband.

I was afraid of being alone.

For a long time, I felt myself leaning on my daughter and her kids. I just couldn't face the real world and I was afraid of being alone and making decisions by myself. I would go to church trying to cope with being alone however, I just couldn't bring myself to go into God's house, because David would not be there with me. I cried all the time behind closed doors and sometimes at work. I stopped going to church a few Sundays; because I couldn't stop crying and feeling sorry for myself. I began to feel that my children and grandchildren didn't love me like they did when my husband was alive because they stop coming over to check on me. The phone calls stop coming and the presence of my friends got shorter. I would spend the night with my daughter a lot and then I started feeling I was in the way. My heart was hurting so bad even when I was with my family, but I didn't want to go home and be alone.

I was afraid of being at home at night.

I felt I had to have family around me.

I felt the need to ask for help making decisions on things my husband did for me.

I was so depended on my husband that I didn't trust myself to make important decisions.

I felt like my self-esteem was at its lowest level. But after many years had gone by, I knew I had to get a grip on my life.

I began reading the bible and talking to God more and remembering what the word of God was saying to me. Then the light came on in my mind and in my heart. I began to realize I was being selfish and was having my own pity parties. I guess I wanted people to feel sorry for me. Then, I realized that God's words told us he would never leave us nor forsake us, especially the widows. I started hearing a soft voice the (Holy Spirit) talking to me. I realized that this was God's decisions to call my husband home and I believe he knows what's best for us. He holds the future for me and I must believe in his decisions. He gave us almost forty years together in marriage which was a blessing. I had to let go and let God have his way in my life. As I attempt to conclude this portion of my journey through life as a widow, I am reminded that God guides us when we must make those tough decisions; about life.

"I am the way, the truth and the life; John 14:6

I was once afraid to make my own decisions but God gave me the courage to step out on his word and know that he is all I need. I am now very active in my walk with God. I began to encourage myself as I remembered this scripture Isaiah 41:10 *"Be not dismayed, for I am thy God, I will strengthen thee."* and Proverb 3:5, *"Trust in the Lord with all your heart, and lean not on your own understanding."*

I began to take care of my own business. I walked into the State Farm Insurance office to update my husband's information. Once there; I met this lady who helped me with updating my profile. She was the director of a widow's ministry. She informed me of the things I needed to get my information updated on my husband records. She also informed me about the widow's ministry and how it would embrace and encourage me through this journey. I don't believe it was a mistake that we came together like that. God put us together and life really changed when I began to do for myself.

Mary encouraged and assured me that I could take care of my personal business instead of always getting someone else to do it for me. She recommended that I connect with Sheila, our president to get professional financial advice. At that point in my life I was afraid to make any decisions because my husband did everything for me, for so many years. However, I found the encouragement and push I needed. After becoming a member of The Next Chapter Widows' Ministry, I felt comfortable in making decisions for myself with the help of God's guidance and the widows' ministry. This ministry taught me how to take charge of my life and make decisions on my own. The ministry has so much to offer a widow during their grieving process. It is the family God has placed me in and we learned from each other's stages of grief. We travel together, go bowling, Valentine and Christmas parties and have a great time. I have increased my activities in keeping my body healthy by joining the Lou Walker Senior Center in Lithonia, Georgia. Meeting so many nice people brightens my day. I am very involved in the Performing Arts Choir, Praise Dance Group, and I love our Bid Whist Card Club.

Listen, my Sisters, this is the door that God has opened for us to travel through. He brought us to it and he will carry us through it. I love it, and like the new person I am now. I enjoy life. Thank you, God, I am so happy! Thank God for "The Next Chapter". This is a place to be. Join us and let's grow together in Jesus Christ.

A Widow's Touch

Life After

Patricia Brown

Decatur, Georgia

I thank God for The Greater Piney Grove Baptist Church. When my husband passed, my church family came immediately, comforting phone calls, visiting with me and getting me up and out of my home. They continued to visit me and they unconditionally took me places I needed go; like a good Christian should do. I thank God for them. Sometimes the days were very hard but that's okay because I know that God was there for me to pick me up when I fall. Becoming a widow was so new for me. When the Lord called my husband home, I wondered?

'WHAT ABOUT ME?'

'WHAT DO I DO, NOW?'

The Lord told me "I will not leave you comfortless: I will come to you." *John 14:18* I am thankful for a mighty God we serve. I love the Lord and I know that he doesn't make mistakes. Weeping may endure for a night but joy comes in the morning. I do miss *Larry*!

A Widow's Touch

I Was Forced to Take Charge

By Rose Bone
Decatur, Georgia

When William transitioned in June 2004, my life changed on so many levels. I asked myself so many times, what's going to happen to me? How am I going to feel without having William to make decisions, talk with, or just how will it feel on the other side of my bed which we shared for thirty-four years? I felt lost. Grieving was something I couldn't do because I was forced to take charge of everything around me and I had no clue on where to start. William was the one that took care of everything. Now it seems like I am drowning. When I stopped trying to fix everything and just surrendered to God that's when I saw His work. He put people in my path for a reason. God reminded me we are never alone.

The first meeting.

I can't remember who brought me to the Next Chapter's meeting. I am so glad that they did, because I met other people that had loss their love ones. I listened to their stories on how they were dealing with grief. God knew I needed to hear their stories. I needed to hear how they received strength to move on and how to be of a moral support to someone else. In

A Widow's Touch

Galatians 6:2, it states, "share each other burdens, and in this way, obey the law of Christ."

God knows what we need, when we need it and how we can bless someone else. I now understand that The Next Chapter was the connection I needed. Here we are working together through various stages of grief. We can help each other with just a kind word or a listening ear. Through it all, God gets the glory.

A Widow's Touch

A Good Samaritan Killed

By Freda Denise Brown
East Point, Georgia

On June 25, 1997, I was on my way to work on highway 75/85 north during the 7:30 a.m. Atlanta's rush hour. I was listening to V103 radio station in the midst of a lot of traffic when the news reporter announced that a good Samaritan was just killed; and he was a firefighter. Immediately, I called fire station #10 and a young man suggested that I speak to his captain. I knew then, that it was my husband, Ernest Brown. I was almost at work and just blocks away from the scene of the accident. Thank God, they had already removed Ernest's body. I saw several firefighters at the scene and one of them drove me home.

My father was there waiting.

Once home, a cluster of firemen was standing in my yard but all I could think of was getting to my children before anyone else told them about the accident. My father, who is now deceased, was there. This was one of the hardest things I ever had to tell my children; they were so distraught. People were everywhere.

However, I was able to get to my bed and I began to pray. I asked God to show me that my husband was in heaven with him. Instantly, I felt peace and a rush of heat from my head to my toes. God helped me through this period and there were so many people, family, friends and even strangers at my home to help.

Fast forward twelve years, March 10, 2009, we are in Intensive Care Medicine (ICM) at Piedmont Hospital in Atlanta with my mother. The doctor called us all to come together. We all gathered around her bed singing, praying and rejoicing when she took her last breath. What an awesome experience that was to watch her transition; especially knowing that beyond a shadow of doubt that she was with God.

October 20, 2010, we are at Atlanta's Medical Hospital, again at 2:00 a.m. – with my father who had just passed away. We were singing, praying and rejoicing only because my father was with the Lord.

March 3, 2011 – we were all at my parent's home in Atlanta, where we had moved my sister so that she could recuperate from a five and ½ month stay in Wellstar Hospital from a major auto accident.

At 5:30 a.m., I received a call from my brother.

When I got to the house, I went into the bedroom to talk to my sister with a cup of ice in my hand. I was showing and speaking tough love so we could get her back to the hospital; however, she was not hearing it. My sister decided to lie on the floor; two minutes later she was gone. Now, she is with the Lord. Too many loses. How do I deal with that? I just didn't become a widow, I became a single parent, too; two new roles. Blissfully,

A Widow's Touch

I'm not going to cry. It has been fourteen years now but it still hurts. God promised in His word that He will never leave us nor forsake us, so even through our toughest trials He will carry us through. When I didn't know what to do during my husband's, parents, and sister's death, God was my sole guide. I promise He will get you through. His love will never leave nor forsake you. Thank you God for sending; "The Next Chapter Widows' Ministry".

A Widow's Touch

Courage and Wisdom

Frances Baskin

Decatur, Georgia

My life's purpose now is to serve God.

Being a widow for five years led to some control of my feelings, and how I deal with the uncertainties of life without my husband. Dwight was very articulate and smart. He was very caring towards our son, daughter, mother, and sisters; before and after our marriage. We were married for thirty-six years; all was not perfect, but sincere. He was a friend and a companion. Dwight had a wide-range of knowledge and skills and he was always available for me.

We both retired.

Dwight retired as an electronic technician and I worked in business administration. He had a great love for computers which he mastered for a long time until his sickness progressed. A pulmonary disease connected to lung cancer took him from me. I knew that he was in God's hand, and that the Lord was in control of it all. I began to rely on Jesus Christ to give me courage to face tomorrow. When I realized he was weakening, we didn't discuss his illness or possibility of death.

A Widow's Touch

We accepted that death was something we all must face. I had to work at finding the courage and wisdom to realize that I needed Jesus Christ; His love and salvation. Now that I am living for Him, I can make it through the next chapter of my life.

He Was Never Sick. He Was Tall, Stocky and Handsome

By Rosa Williams
Decatur, Georgia

When we got the report that my husband had inoperable lung cancer, my world collapsed. Bill was never sick, he was tall, stocky and handsome. He had the personality that kept me and other people laughing. We dated four years. Our marriage was a gift for thirty-six years. And Bill gave me two beautiful children. We had such a romantic courtship that I smile every time I think about it. Bill was the type of husband that kissed me when he came in and when he left. He sent flowers, cards for all occasions. He also bought most of my clothes because he had great taste and he didn't penny pinch; like me.

He always treated me like a lady.

I would walk into our bedroom and clothes would be laid out all over the bed. He always treated me like a lady. We were in sync so often, at times we would start a thought of a great vacation spot and before we realized it we would be creating new memories. We didn't argue much because he would just leave, you can't argue by yourself. He only had a few family members but we were all there to escort him to the doctor, just looking for some sign of hope. We went through chemo and radiation and tried everything we could but he passed before Easter while at home. I was so relieved that I didn't have to put him into a hospice hospital.

I just wanted to die, too.

I ached to the core. I could not see how I could ever live without him. It took over five years to get my legs back because I felt my other leg had been amputated. I didn't feel right being alone. I had never even thought about being without my husband and I couldn't stop crying. It just drove me to utter despair. When I saw other couples together, I asked; "why him and why me"?

The calls stop after the funeral and people move on with their lives. They have no idea of the agony that goes on and on within you. So, I kept showing up as usual but sometimes I could not conceal or contain my grief. Then I asked for prayer because everyone seemed so far away.

Thank God for the State Insurance Commissioner.

As the oldest in my family; I was trying to keep everything at home together. My family had no clue about the depth of my despair or the financial situations I faced. An example of my stress was; when I got into a battle with the medical insurance company, after they had denied all my claims. The State Insurance Commissioner, gave me immediate and personal assistance. He was a Godsend who made the insurance company pay the claims. The commissioner also got the insurance company to assign a personal contact agent at their company for any additional problems that might occur.

A Widow's Touch

What a relief!

I was afraid when I saw the medicals bills coming in and I was only working part time. Next came the problems with the Internal Revenue Service. My name was on my husband's business and we filed income taxes together. I knew nothing about doing taxes, especially corporate taxes. For the last two years, we completely relied on an accountant to submit our taxes and I thought that everything was in order. However, eventually my home was in jeopardy. Gaining control of my finances was very costly. Again, I felt so scared and helpless.

Even our experienced tax attorney failed me. A few years later, I learned that I could get assistance from the State & Federal Tax Revenue office. At this point, I was able to work through the situations. I must say I learned a lot in this process about our business. There were so many details and decisions to be made before and after at a time when I was clearly not in my right mind. During this time, I had two horrible nights that I have never described to anyone.

Why is it that things happen in the middle of the night?

No one to call or actually no one could help with what was going on. I felt so helpless but I could do what I needed to do. I learned the meaning of 'when you are weak, then you are strong'. God was right there, holding me up, giving me directions and the strength to keep going on. My strength was unreal.

I sat in church many days, dreading the service to end. I didn't want to go to an empty house. I tried to use the resources from my grief classes but there were no sessions near my home. I enjoyed traveling across town to a Hospice Center to participate in the group sessions they offered for widows. I didn't know any widows; so being able to interact with other survivors at the center was extremely helpful. I learned from the widows as they shared their different stages of grief. I often wondered how they could go on. It was the only place I felt comfortable.

I made reservations for one!

I felt like an odd ball when I went out. One Sunday after leaving church, I decided that I wanted to go out to eat. I couldn't reach anyone; I got depressed. Out of the blue, my phone rang. It was a long-distance call from one of my husband's friends. He had lost his wife some years earlier. I didn't tell him anything about my not finding anyone to dine with me.

However, in our short conversation, he said, "you know you going to have to get use to going places by yourself". Later that day, I made reservation for one, at a country estate restaurant. I arrived one hour later, the waiter gave me a nice little private table at a window. I pretended my husband was with me. The rest is history. Now, I travel the U.S. and internationally with a variety of interesting people.

Another experience that I overcame was panicking when anything went wrong with my car or my home. Repairs can be quite costly and I didn't know who to trust. Some service people take advantage of women and seniors. Trying to find someone who is both reliable and affordable is an ongoing task. It's equally disappointing to have to pay someone every time something must be done. So many amazing things happened during my husband's illness and consequent demise.

I felt God's power, provision and protection. He literally carried me through.

It was not easy to adjust to the single life after forty years with the same man. It was a little over five years before I was forced to make a decision about maintaining my health. I had to look at what I had left. It was important to get out of the house. I would do strange things like smelling his hats. I had a girlfriend that stood by me. She was a volunteer usher at different art venues so she took me to one and I got hooked. I started working at plays, concerts, all over Atlanta. She also had a vacation timeshare unit and she would keep after me until I agreed to go with her. I always enjoyed myself but my first answer was no in many instances. Now, I love to travel and to gain new experiences. I am active in different ministries at church and a member of a vibrant, state of the art senior center.

I am now opened to new male friendships.

It's been eleven years and I am comfortable with who I am. I do get lonely sometimes on holidays, birthday, anniversaries, but it's getting less intense. I had not been in a relationship for many years, I resisted all opportunities that came my way. Now I am opened to new male friendships, but not just any man. I was already engaged at the time I met my husband Bill and he too, was a Godsend. So, I am confident that God can do it again, if it's His will for me. Otherwise, I have many wonderful memories and somehow, I feel that Bill is still with me.

I am a testimony to God's goodness and love. I am willing to share that love and support with others going through the storm. God said, "I will never leave you nor forsake you". This gives me the confidence to go on. I've emerged as a stronger person and I am grateful for the time we spent together. It was a lonely journey, and I felt no one could understand my pain and I certainly couldn't explain it. I used to leave church and go to the Hospice Center. There I felt comforted being around others going through the same thing. When I joined The Next Chapter Widows' Ministry, I felt that same level of comfort. I received great support, new relationships, opportunity to travel and all the different group activities. My spiritual and personal growth came from the fellowship and group sessions they offer.

Three Enemies That I Wasn't Expecting Came Along for the Ride

By Tania Boyd-Hill
Lithonia, Georgia

Fast forward to now...and remembering.

On August 4, 2001, my life changed!

For me a family vacation had turned into a slow-motion picture. At thirty-eight years, old with two children, my daughter three and my son seven, I became a widow. Today, my son is twenty-one, in college, majoring in electrical engineering, and my daughter is seventeen, a senior in high school, an avid soccer player, while pondering over which college to attend.

My college sweetheart.

John, my husband of twelve and a half years, my college sweetheart, and on that August day he was a groomsman in my brothers' wedding; he died of a heart disease; a heart attack. John was only thirty-eight years old. I know you might be thinking how sad. Yet, on a positive note, we were surrounded by family and friends on such an occasion. Before my husband

75

died, even though I was saved, active in church, and a Sunday School attendee, I was still living an independent life and relied on my own strength for many things. Losing John made me realize that I needed to do more work on my relationship with Christ, and I needed to learn more about how to depend on Him for strength.

I learned a lot about grief.

I experienced grief, like all of you have, but with me, three enemies that I wasn't expecting came along for the ride. They were anxiety, depression and fear. I've never experienced these before. In my distress, I sought out Christian grief counseling, support from family and friends, lay counseling and medication. I learned a lot about grief; but the most important thing I learned was that "Christ is the Answer".

My Christian grief counselor told me that if I was closer to God, this grief experience wouldn't have been so very, very, difficult. Initially, the first three months of counseling, I sat there with the counselor, and did not speak. During this time, I was given many scriptures, but these two impacted me the most. The first one was told to me by my widow friend, Mary.

"Fear thou not; for I am with thee: be not dismayed, for I am thy God: I will strengthen thee; I will help thee; I will uphold thee." Isaiah 41:10

"Yea, though I walk through the valley of the shadow of death, I will fear no evil: for thou art with me." Psalm 23:4

(The keyword is through—you go through, but you keep pushing forward no—place to rest for a long period of time.)

Grief is a roller coaster, but believe me, it does smooth out.

A Widow's Touch

Once, while attending Christian grief counseling, my counselor told me, she wanted me to get to the point where I was flying like a bird, living, taking care of myself and my children. At the time, I thought she was crazy. Just as she told me, life got back to normal, and I was doing things with my kids. The first major thing was going out to the movies. We even took a picture together that evening, and visits to my husband's grave with them was comforting.

I began flying like a bird. I had lost a lot of weight and was looking good! To this day, I am still flying like a bird. I am now a high school teacher. Several years later, a widow friend of mine shared this scripture, and to this day, it is so real and relevant; as each day, we are living and growing older.

Isaiah 46:4 (NIV) reads: "And even to your old age and gray hairs, I am He; I am He who will sustain you. I have made you and I will carry you; I will sustain you and I will rescue you."

Yet again, during this time, I had to start getting trained by God all over again. My kids and I returned to Sunday School. I was learning again that spending time with God and Bible Study was essential. Being a part of the body of Christ is a vital part of recovery. We learned that Christ is the answer. During the summer of 2005, I was visited by grief after a long absence. I prayed like never before. I've learned that my loved one, your loved ones, are asleep in Jesus. Yes, death is final here on earth. But, it is also a comma. We believers will be reunited with them in glory. Let your life, be dependent on God.

A Widow's Touch

Mourn and Move On!

By Diedre Adams
Clermont, Florida

Synopsis of: Weddings, Wheelchairs and Widowhood

All marriages have some imperfections. My marriage was definitely no different, it was damaged with pain and many deficiencies. When most people mourn, they tend to forget the bad and focus on the good. However, the journey that Albert and I traveled was quite a bumpy road. I was left exhausted and burnt out after twelve-years of chronic illnesses and extensive home care.

It's now many months after Albert's death and I wish I could say that it was easy for me to remember the word 'us' the way we were; when we first married. It was hard to separate the previous experiences of harsh feelings from the man that he became. The stark realism of the loss was so hard to bear as I reminisced through my years of marriage, I thought that I needed to heal. It was just so hard that I couldn't just *mourn and move on.*

First, let me make a disclaimer because in order to share my story, I must reveal elements of our life which may cast my husband in poor light. This is not my intention or desire. I want to sincerely inspire and help others *mourn and move on.*

My husband Albert had a kidney disease since childhood. The disease led to a horrific stroke and multiple other issues. Albert was on dialysis treatments for over 30 years. However, he was a man 100%!

The emotional devastation of chronic illness overwhelmed him and spilled out into our marriage in a caustic and harmful way. The result was a backlash of emotional toxic waste. This was what the Spirit of God had to clean up so that I could *mourn and move on.*

In 2010, something changed about Albert. He tried expressing more loving and caring behaviors toward me. After, he was placed in a nursing home, I made an effort to see him, daily. Even with that, my long-term damaged heart was not ready to accept what God had done with Albert in those recent months. The Lord was preparing to take him home and had softened and restored his spirit. At this point, Albert had faced the reality of his situation and gained peace in God. He had *mourned* and was ready to *move on.*

I was still in another place. The results of our imperfect marriage had caught up with me and left me unable to receive affectionate expressions from him. As a loving wife who had been so broken-down, I wouldn't allow the walls of my defenses be reached. I loved him, but I didn't want to be hurt again. My emotions were shielded and guarded. We functioned; but did not flourish. I prayed for God to sooth Albert's emotional pain as he suffered through his illness. He was angry and often directed his rage at me. God, didn't give up on him, I was just too exhausted to see that I was witnessing the results of many prayers. The miracle was right there before me and I didn't recognize it. Then Albert was gone. So, I was left to mourn before I could move on.

Albert's passing was so much harder than I expected. Now, my thoughts are; I believed that God could have miraculously touched Albert's body. God could have healed him; God could have gotten Albert up and walked him away from the dialysis bed, forever. And He could have wiped away all his chronic illnesses. The reality I had to face was, his choices were to be healed or accept death and go home to God. Years later, those possibilities were still hanging over my head. The reality of death was a tremendous blow. So, I mourned and could not move on, not just yet.

As time passed, I continued to play scenes of our life together over and over in my head. Then, something astounding began to happen. I started analyzing and dissected things from our past with more clarity. It was refreshing that I could think. The exhaustion was gone and I could think. God revealed more and more of what the process did for both us. Finally, I was mourning with the purpose to move on.

In the midst of God's process, He spoke to me through three passages of scriptures about David's life. First, II Samuel 12:16 and 18. David was losing a son to illness as a result of him falling into sin. While the child was yet sick, he laid before God all night upon the earth. And it came to pass that on the seventh day the child died. David thought that perhaps God would change his mind and heal the child. This is where God directed my attention to II Samuel 12:20, "Then David rose from the earth, and washed, and anointed himself, and changed his apparel, and came into the house of the Lord and worshipped". This passage was significant while Albert was alive. In addition to being full of disease, we allowed sin into our midst and because I didn't stay in a place of continual prayer, I was weary and exhausted! The enemy entered by strife and railed us against each other. Bitterness, hurt and disappointment were the fruit.

As I looked back, I mourned the potential of what our marriage could have been. Our life together was like that of an undeveloped child. Our connection as husband and wife never reached maturity. We couldn't stand on our own or together, we couldn't figure out how to be a blessing to each other or how to create a lasting spiritual legacy that we could leave for those we loved. These are the things I cried and mourned over while dealing with the loss of Albert. I grieved over the misplaced opportunity to enjoy a happy and functional marriage to glorify God. The key message in the midst of this scripture was that my marriage bond was over. Literally, David was able to change his position and stand up and go about his life. Figuratively and spiritually, now God was instructing me to do the same. As time passed, God was urging me to *mourn and move on.*

David's whole countenance changed. He had sobered and learned his lesson and knew that God continued to be his source of strength and comfort. He did what he knew to do from the days of his youth. David worshipped. After reflecting on David's life, I took the time again, to examine my past. I decided to apply the lessons to my current situation and mourned it fully. I was done.

A Widow's Touch

I had mourned, next I had to move on.

In the next season, I began asking the Father how I needed to proceed so that our past lives would not have been in vain. I wanted guidance on how to give God the glory as I embrace the life that's ahead of me. God showed me David in another phase of his life in I Samuel, Chapter 30. David's enemies laid waste to his household and stole his spouses and kidnapped his children. He was a great warrior who had seen many battles but this was just too much for him. David wept until he could weep no more! All that was dear to him was loss. He was in a state of distress because of the expectations of the people around him. He wanted to excel and not fail for the sake of their legacy in their children.

While I mourned, I saw how the enemy laid waste to my house and destroyed our testimony. Those that were supposed to build us up had failed because of our self-interest. Our legacy was captured and bound and in the midst of it all; I had lost my spouse. Over those challenging months, I wept until I could weep no more. My sorrow was complete and real. Then like David in I Samuel 30:6; "David encouraged himself in the Lord his God". He remembered and kept forefront in his mind that the LORD is his God!

Hence, I encouraged myself with worship, songs, and learned to delight in His word more than ever before. As David put on the ephod, he knew where his direction for victory would come from. What he heard from the people kept him in a place of distress but God pointed David in a new direction. Like David, I had mourned and now I needed to know where to move on, too.

A Widow's Touch

God's words were clear to David in I Samuel 30:8. He answered him, *"Pursue: for thou shalt surely overtake them and without fail recover all."* In the next season, God did allow and encouraged me to *move on.*

He began to bring me into a season where I was recovering. The enemies spoil was mine as well. God's plan was to allow for this season to be one of recompense from all the devastation of the enemy, but to reap benefits, I had to move in the direction God was showing me.

God did miraculous things.

In the last two years, God has done miraculous things in my life. But I had to experience the loss of my husband to understand the impact of the grieving process. It was important for me to understand grief on all the different levels to be able to free the baggage. I can say that I loved my husband I will hold on to the good times we shared. I have laid the hurts and disappointments to rest with him. God has given me a new chapter of healing and wholeness.

My life today is more marvelous than I could ever have imagined. The time of mourning was well spent in coming through the wilderness and growing into the greatness that God has planned for me. I am also sure that Albert would have wanted this for me, as well. *I have Mourned and Moved On!*

A Widow's Touch

I Learned How to Manage My Life

By Helen Hurst
Lithonia, Georgia

The death of my husband Johnny, my best friend brought me to a place I did not think I could handle. My husband was a fun-loving guy, one of the good old boys, very thoughtful, and he took care of his family as best he could. He would allow me to buy nice things and he took care of everything. Johnny kissed me every morning before he left for work. He was the kind of person you could not push around, I respected him for that. His style, let me and everyone else know he was the man of the house. On the other side, he was not the most romantic person. Every year on our anniversary, we would have champagne and toast each other.

I totally depended on him.

When my mother passed, Johnny was at my side in every way possible. As in every marriage, there was good time and bad times, but the good outweighed the bad. The day, my husband died the world stopped. I did not know which way to go or turn. Then, I remembered that God did not bring me this far to leave me. So, I did what I had to do, I called the appropriate people and notified everyone concerned. Then, I had to think what I would do with my life since my best friend was gone. The first decisions I made was to sell our house and moved to another part of town. I changed my church membership. I learned quickly how to manage my life around things that were driven by my marriage. When Johnny was here, many times I got so angry at small insignificant things. And many times, I would ask God, why He took Johnny out of my life?

Although, I am an outgoing person and fun loving, I get sad and feel so all alone, even in the middle of a crowd. I would go to work and see something or hear something and I would cry, cry, and cry. I would cry until the end of the day. Then, I would leave work and put my sunglasses on and walk into a store like nothing ever happen.

This was a process I repeated, often. But it got better and I remembered one thing; God did not bring me this far to leave me. I started leaning and depending on God, for everything.

I asked God to put the right person in my life.

Going out with my girlfriends and to restaurants by myself made me feel uncomfortable. Mostly, because I couldn't stop crying. I think that somehow, I am comparing Johnny, my loving husband to my friends; because I know how capable my husband was. I put my best foot forward and ask God to show me the way. It is getting better and better but I will always have some little thing that we did together that would bring a smile to my face.

Johnny wasn't very starry-eyed but we would go on vacation together. One year we wanted to go to New York City, since he had promised me, that he would take me back to see Niagara Falls.

A Widow's Touch

He died before he could keep that promise.

Later, I went to Niagara Fall with my church. The whole time there, I thought about how good it would have been to have Johnny by my side. I am still alone, but I try not to be lonely. I am now involved with my church and my community center. I go out with my girlfriends and have a great time. God left me here for a reason and a purpose. I want to fulfill my life and be the best mother, grandmother and friend that I can be.

A Widow's Touch

The Lord Brought Me Through

By Eva Turner
Lithonia, Georgia

The year of 2006 started out to be a very good year. Life with my husband, Alvin, was very good. As soon as spring arrived, he started planning our annual vacation for either June or July. He always frolicked with which month was best, and it never mattered to me. My husband was very detailed oriented; all I had to say is "yes" I want to go. I would gladly pack my bags for where ever we decided to go. I was never disappointed on the vacations we took. I always looked forward to this time of the year. Alvin spent much of his adult life in the military and traveled extensively throughout his career. It was easier for him to work out all the details for our vacation; things like hotel reservations and travel routes. He would take care of everything and he enjoyed planning our trips as much I enjoyed going.

He would brush everything off as being something temporary.

However, this year instead of going on our vacation, Alvin was forced to seek medical attention. He had discovered that after a brief walk or just climbing a short flight of stairs, he would have difficulty breathing. He rarely went to see the doctor for regular check-ups. No matter how many discussions we had on the subject. He would just brush everything off as being something temporary; even though his difficulty breathing did not go away. He finally consented to be taken to a doctor. We learned that there was a problem with his prostate. While he was being considered for surgery, his x-rays revealed an aneurysm in his stomach. This would require an emergency by-pass surgery that was estimated to last about three hours but instead turned into a seven-hour operation.

That was the beginning of a cycle that never ended.

There were so many complications. The shortness of breath that brought him to the doctor in the first place turned out to be pneumonia in both lungs. With everything else that was going on, he exasperated twice and required life support. After so many struggling days he was given a trachea, oxygen and a feeding tube. He spent a month in ICU going from one complication to another.

Still with all of this going on, he rarely complained. He only asked for pain relievers when it became unbearable. Finally, he could be moved to a rehabilitation center for what supposed to have last no longer than thirty days, this was comforting to hear. But as time passed, Alvin was getting restless. He began to ask for foods he could not eat or liquids that he could not swallow. He also wanted to go for walks so I took him outside and pushed him around in the parking lot in a wheel chair. I knew he was tired of the facility and being away from home for so long. I understood his loneliness and his quiet fear of the unknown. So, I was sure to visit him every day bringing him items from home so he would not feel so misplaced and alone. During his illness, his mind was still very sharp. He was curious about everything and excited thinking about what he would do when he was released from the hospital. I would tell him current events and talk about any and everything for his enjoyment, I taught him how to cap his trachea so that he could talk and that made him happy. He could not wait for me to get there each day so that he could tell me what happened or about something that he had seen on television. I was pleased and saw some real progress for a little while. Then something happened. I arrived one morning and he was still in bed too weak to even sit up. After getting over my initial shock, I found the doctor who told me that his cancer had spread throughout his organs.

We were Christians and we believed that God is a miracle worker.

When we were told that Alvin was diagnosed with prostate cancer that was attacking his organs. We both knew what the end results would be; but we were always praying and hoping for a miracle. We prayed that God would heal him, if it was "His Will". We left it entirely in His hands. We also knew that it was not the will of God to heal everyone and if He didn't, it was not because He couldn't. It was just not "His Will". We silently accepted "God's Will" and went on doing what had to be done each day.

Alvin's days started to play out like a roller coaster. One day he would sit up most of the day. The next day, he would want to stay in bed. I couldn't say I knew how he felt because I didn't. I could only imagine and I tried my best to make sure that he was clean, comfortable and was not in pain.

It was so very painful watching him deteriorate.

A Widow's Touch

By the third month, things seemed to be going downhill fast. Nothing was helping. Alvin seemed to be losing weight by the minute. One morning, he just could not become fully awake. He slept continuously for three whole days. His doctor called me out of the room and told me that they were discontinuing all services. There was nothing else to be done. His cancer was attacking his brain. I was told to make arrangements for him to be transferred to Hospice care. I made the arrangements but he didn't make it. That same evening after arriving home and minutes after closing my door, his doctor called with the announcement that no one wants to hear.

"Mrs. Turner, I'm sorry to inform you that Mr. Turner just passed away. Where do you want us to send his body?"

I believed she said that all in one sentence. I must have given her an answer. I can't believe what's happening right now. I'm standing in the middle of the floor talking to myself. "Did that doctor say he passed away?"

"What do I do now? I need to call someone, my family, his family, my church's bereavement committee." "What?"

After a call to my daughter, everyone just took over and made life so much easier for me throughout the planning and actual funeral services. Deeply grieved, I simply went through the motions. Alvin was gone and all hopes of him ever coming home again were gone. Everything in my life would be different. From day one, I felt the void. I thank God for family and friends. Someone was physically at my house day and night for many weeks that followed.

After everyone had gone, however, reality set in. I am alone, so now what? I would ask myself. The house has only one occupancy now and it was so very quiet. The words, I will have to go it alone now kept flowing through my head. As for the house, I had no trouble taking care of it and keeping things running smoothly. I had done so for the past four months. But it was all the things that Al and I did together that I was going to miss. Alvin had been a fun-loving person who had enjoyed making my life easy. We liked doing things and going places together. We had gotten to the point of just enjoying life.

My biggest challenge was trying to sleep at night.

The minute that I would close my eyes, it was as if someone had put a movie on to play. The scenes were things that had happened over the last four months; Alvin's suffering, his surgeries, being attached to his oxygen, and the tubular feeding. I would recall how, although, he seldom complained, sometimes he would cry. All of this I had witnessed daily and now it seemed to be embedded in my brain. Some nights I got very little sleep. While listening to the movie re-play in my head. I would pray that God would take control and bring peace to my spirit and restore my joy. I continued to pray the same prayer every night knowing that He had heard me the first time. Yet, it brought me some comfort. Things remained the same for a while longer. I felt that I was at the point of total exhaustion. Then one night, after retiring to bed and waiting for the movie in my head to start, I waited and waited. But nothing happened. The movie didn't start. I fell asleep and slept all night and the movie hasn't played again since. I thank God for peace.

Now it was time to face reality.

A Widow's Touch

When I looked out of my window, the world seemed gloomy. The day was rainy and cold and I thought I would feel so much better if the sun was shining. I needed more time to adjust to this new life and wasn't sure what it was going to take for me to get there. Then I realized, I can't make it happen. I need to wait on the Lord and just give it time. I knew that I had, even said this to someone else, when they were in this position. So, I resigned myself to taking life one day at a time. One day, everything would be quiet and lonely with just me alone with my thoughts and memories.

The next day, I might hear about an event that my husband and I used to attend and now everyone was invited, except me. Maybe I was overlooked when I was supposed to help coordinate a certain program. You find yourself slowly but surely feeling as though you were being shifted to the outer edge. I know nothing was done viciously. People just don't quite know what to do when you become a widow – especially when you're the only widow in the group that you interact with most often. I slowly found myself withdrawing from things that I once liked to do or places I had gone to before. I was learning to accept life for what it is and how to carve out my own niche.

I joined new organizations and ministries. The Next Chapter Widows' Ministry was truly a Godsend. I have met some very nice people that I feel so comfortable being around. We all have a different story but the end results are the same; we are widows.

We can uplift one another.

A Widow's Touch

The blessing that we can share, as our lives continue and we realize that he is no longer here, is we can find comfort in knowing that our loved ones are in a better place, just waiting for our arrival. In the meantime, we are to enjoy every moment of the love God's granted us. And live guiltlessly happy and be thankful that our loved ones were in our lives. Also, the happiness they brought to us, if only for a time. I am very thankful for the ministry, but more thankful to God, He always sends us what we need when we need it. Everything is in His time and always right on time. While I would not have chosen Alvin's departure from my life, I know that my loved one was a God-fearing man of faith; he has gone on to a better place. His long-term suffering has ended. While I still missed him terribly, I have learned that pain and sorrow endures only for a night but joy truly does come in the morning.

There is a different movie that plays in my head, now. One of expectancy for each day I am granted. I can smile again, and laugh, without the tears. I can share my story with others while at the same time find comfort when they share their experiences with me. I am learning one day at a time how to live by – treasuring all the memories. Now, I'm able to expect more for my future. I thank God now just for life itself but especially for giving me a man like Alvin to love.

A Widow's Touch

My Traveling Buddy is Gone

By W. Esther Woods
Decatur, Georgia

I was born in a small town in Tuscaloosa, Alabama. When I was young my parents had strict rules about the activities that I could participate in. However, it was alright for me to go to our town's pint-size happenings with my brother, his classmates and best friends. My parents seemed to think that one of my brother's friend's named Willie "Bill" Woods was a nice young man. He was very respectful and from a good family. His uncle Silas Woods was the pastor of our local church. Bill and I had a few things in common. We sang in the school choir and we were in the same Sunday School class. I felt he acted a little slow and he didn't talk much. I went out with him to see movies, a few dances, several ball games and of course we were at church together. We dated for three years before we got married.

We often talked about moving away from our first home in Alabama and then an opportunity came. The small printing company that Bill worked for moved to Bronx, New York. The company's owner asked my husband to transfer with his family to New York. Bill had recently become his newest certified printer. Bill worked hard on his job and in the evenings, he went to night school. He was happy that the hours he spent getting certified, paid off. He felt proud to be able to provide a better life for his family. It was very hard for a while adjusting to the lifestyle of the Northerners, but, I am grateful for the change. We received a lot of support and we experienced many new things we would not have gotten exposed to in the South. At the time, I found a job working to nine every night at a chronic disease hospital as a Certified Nursing Assistance. We raised two girls Pamela and Patricia in New York and kept them very active in school. We did a lot of traveling and even went abroad to England, as a family. Both daughters graduated from high school and college. My oldest daughter Pamela is a Licensed Practical Nurse. Patricia is Founder & Editor of her own company. The two of them blessed us with six beautiful grandchildren.

We had a good life.

We had a good life with struggles but made it through with God's help. Later, we moved back south to Atlanta and we had to make several new life style adjustments. The first one was due to Bill's diabetic illness, which he's had ever since he was thirty-seven years old. Even knowing of his health concerns, he didn't follow his recommended diet.

In 1997 and three years after moving to Georgia, he had heart surgery. However, after he recovered he was able to return to work. Later, my mother had a stroke and came to live with us. I would take her home to Alabama on weekends so she could attend church service and fellowship. At times, I would cry and pray about this situation but later a family member decided to move in with my mother and took care of her daily needs. Bill's eye vision began to worsen. He lost his sight in one eye which caused him to be placed on disability. Later, he had to go on dialysis treatment and he also was not able to drive himself for treatment, anymore. God gave us strength each day and a strong caring group of supporting family members and friends. Bill realized that his health was not getting better. However, we continued to have faith in God and we kept attending church. We were also blessed to be able to keep up with our visits to my mother's home in Alabama. In 2001, he began to stay at home, not eating or taking his medicine or forgetting. Bill became weaker in his legs and they start swelling. He had a vascular bye-pass on his leg and six weeks later a pacemaker. After all of this, Bill was feeling better and he was showing signs of hope and optimisms.

Thank God our financial situation was in good condition.

On April 5, 2002 at the early age of sixty-three, Bill passed away. From the beginning, Bill always stressed the importance of living on a family budget. I learned so much from him and I continue today using the financial skills he taught me. I will always give him full credit for keeping us money-wise and sound. I am thankful to God for His love for us and the strength He gave me. Because our financial situation was in fairly good condition, I started attending hospice family support groups. I met widows and other families that had lost love one's. Listening and sharing some of our memories and plans from day to day gave comfort to me in many ways.

Three months later, I started attending regularly the senior group fellowships at my church. I enjoyed the meetings and the day trips as well as the weekly activities. I joined another ministry and continue to visit my mother, more often. I kept myself busy and had my moments grieving and crying. When you are hurting, sleeping when you are tired, eating when you are hungry or sneezing when you nose itches, these are all natural ways of healing a broken heart.

God gave me peace.

These last thirteen years, I am thankful I know God and He was with me every step of the way during all the struggles, trial and tribulations, and in my weakest points in my faith walk. Many times after Bill's transition, getting home in a hurry became a habit, knowing that no one would be there to talk to me, it was comforting, at first. This habit took a long time to break. I am grateful to God that He gave me peace, courage and the wisdom to know the difference. I always celebrate special days of the year that remind me of the special people, I love–present or past. My mother passed two years later in March 2004. I am truly grateful for all the support I received from family and friends during my trying times.

A Widow's Touch

He Was Warned That His Liver Would Fail

By Margaret Jackson
Lithonia, Georgia

My husband Ralph passed on September 16, 2007. On one hand, it feels like yesterday, but on the other hand I feel more distant from the grief and I look back to those days with less pain. My husband's death was not a sudden death where he died without warning. He had been diagnosed with a terminal illness and died in hospice. He had been warned that his liver would fail. I prayed that God would take his craving for alcohol away.

Years of in and out of the hospital.

Ralph was not able to conquer his alcoholism. This illness is painful not only for the ill person, but also the caregiver and/or supporter who must watch them gradually wasting away. We went through years of him going in and out of the hospital. It was taking a toll on me. When he was taken away, I said that God took him away so that I could live. The death of a mate is unmatched for its emptiness and profound sadness. My loss and grief that accompanied it was very personal, different from

101

anyone else. One minute I'm okay and next I'm in tears. Losing a partner is devastating.

He left our house walking.

Ralph's last trip to the hospital to see the doctor revealed that his liver was 80% non-functional. He left our house walking and Thursday he was connected to a bundle of tubes. At the end of that day things had worsen. By Friday, we were makings plans to transfer Ralph to hospice care. Our family came to see him at the hospital to say "Goodbye". He was sent to hospice later, that Friday afternoon. I visited him that Saturday and Sunday. After being home about twenty-minutes on Sunday evening, hospice called me saying that I needed to come back to the care center.

When I got there they gave me a list of the things that showed that Ralph was transitioning. Sadly, some of his symptoms I had seen on the hospital's list, earlier. As other family members arrived I told them that it was okay to let Ralph go, I shared how I loved him. I had feelings of relief because my loved ones had also been suffering from watching Ralph endure heavy pain on top of his sadness that he couldn't change anything. I truly, wanted him to live a long and good life, but that was no longer an option. At hospice, where my husband passed, just as they provided care and comfort for him, they provided continued support for me through that times of grief and loss. They understand how to comfort, shed light and hold your hand.

For over a year, I received quarterly newsletters dealing with grief and loss issues, information about support group, memorial service visits and phone calls from bereavement staff and trained volunteers, as needed.

A long grieving process is not healthy.

I used professional counseling twice. It was good to hear that all my feelings were normal and what many widows experience. It's good also to cry and rant with others. After I thought I was ready, I made plans to volunteer at the hospice center, but they moved, so I continued to usher at my church. Now it's like what else can I do? I continue to challenge myself to find new things to do. I don't like getting up speaking but I've got to do something to reach out and minister to others, now that I know what it's like to lose your mate. A week or so, after Ralph passed; the calls stopped. It got awfully, lonely. I said; "I know what I'll do. I'll make a list of those I know who have lost their mate and I'll call them every week." I went way back as far as ten years or longer to create my list.

I keep adding to the list.

Because, I know how widow's felt and even what they still feel. I continued to do this and call most of them every Wednesday. I keep adding to the list. I added widowers, those who have lost other relatives and the sick and shut in. When I don't get them on the phone, some will call me. I call even when I don't feel good because I know I am making them feel good. They say; "you sound so good and sweet". One Wednesday, when I returned from my trip to South Africa exhausted, I called a few people. We must remember God has a plan for our lives. (Jeremiah 29:11)

Even through my brokenness and loneliness, I thought about others who were experiencing the loss of a love one. I think about when the pastor and others pray they mention the sick and shut in. Most of them do get well. What about us widows and widowers? We will never get our mates back. Some of us never get over the grief. We are often not mentioned.

I rely on my faith.

We will get through it. We must give each other love and support. Sharing our loss with others, helps. While we feel that no one else is experiencing what we are, it's more likely there are others with similar situations. You come to realized that you don't have to grieve alone. After joining "The Next Chapter Widows' Ministry" I found widows to reach out to and a support group, as well. I have enjoyed the fellowship with the widows through meetings, entertainment, engaging in special projects and traveling.

"I am here to hold a hand and comfort a soul."

A Widow's Touch

My Name is Victory

By Brenda Newsome
Stone Mountain, Georgia

"A new heart also will I give you, and a new spirit will I put within you: and I will take away the stony heart out of your flesh, and I will give you a heart of flesh." Ezekiel 36:26

I became a widow at the age of forty-nine. I now have: three adult daughters, one adult son and a total of five grandchildren, three grandsons and two granddaughters. Albert, my husband and I shared thirty-one years of marriage. Throughout those years, we learned to trust God and place Him as head of our lives. We renewed our vows at twenty-five years of marriage, not expecting God to call him home six years later. All the signs were there; I just never saw them until it was too late.

Each loss is different.

It's funny how we take our loved ones for granted, expecting them to be here for us always. After experiencing the loss of family members such as grandmother, aunts, uncles, cousins and friends, I thought I was prepared for any loss. But how many of you know that each loss is different?

A Widow's Touch

You see, Albert was my high school sweetheart. He was my soul mate. We became serious when I was in the tenth grade and he was preparing to graduate. Al, enlisted in the Navy and asked me to wait on him. Although I said yes, I didn't realize the severity of his questions and what it meant. The only thing I knew was that I loved him and have loved him ever since I was in sixth grade. Early in our marriage we weathered some storms, some ups and downs, taking each other for granted. Sometime even wishing we were never married. When the thought of Albert not being in my life cross my mind, it made me shudder. I remember having a dream he died about two years before he went home to be with the Lord. I could not wake up out of the dream. I was crying in my sleep and pleading with God.

Waking up from the dream.

Finally, waking up from the dream–it took me a minute to get myself together, but I began to thank God that it was only a dream. Later, that day at choir rehearsal I testified how much I love Albert and how we tend to take our love one's for granted, thinking they are always going to be here. If I can say one thing for sure, we loved and had the utmost respect for each other. On the day of his departure, October 31, 2005, although it was Halloween, it was to me an ordinary day. We did not recognize or honor Halloween. Albert worked the night shift and I worked during the day. I kissed him goodbye that morning and went to work.

Because my husband was so tired when he came in that morning, I decided to let him sleep and not to wake him. That afternoon because the trick-or-treaters were out, I decided to work late, just until the children were off the streets.

A Widow's Touch

I thought he was just being cranky.

Once I got home, Albert was lying across the bed not feeling well. He stated that his back and mouth was hurting. After being home for about an hour, he got up to get ready for work. He started ironing his pants and complaining about having holes in them. You must understand my husband worked with batteries and when he would go fishing, he would handle batteries, too. Sometime he had problems with the battery acid eating holes in his cloth.

But this particular day he became upset and accused me of the bleaching holes in his jeans. I pointed out to him if it was bleach there would be white spots around the holes. As of this day I thank the Holy Spirit – for giving me the right words to say. I did not go on into that argument with him even though I wanted to. I felt like telling him to wash his own clothes.

However, I stated; "please do not leave here upset". In fact, in my meekest voice, I suggested he should try washing his clothes for a little while. "The children and I do not have that problem with our cloths." We started laughing and playing after he thought about what I said. The last funny thing he told me was, "I better learn how to drop it like it's hot". That was our little inside joke.

I went down stairs to prepare his lunch. Later, Albert came down stairs and asked me if we had milk. I answered yes, and he ran back upstairs to get his pain medication to take before leaving for work. The last facial expression my youngest daughter saw on her father face was an expression of anguish and distress.

The call.

A Widow's Touch

Albert, came back into the kitchen, took his medication, grabbed his lunch and kissed me good-bye, stating; "I will see you in the morning". About thirty minutes later I received a call from his supervisor asking if my husband was sick. I stated no, he only complained about his back and mouth hurting. Then his supervisor told me that he was unconscious and they could not bring him to. I told my two youngest children to grab their coats so we could go to see about their dad. Nervous, not knowing what to expect while driving and praying, when we got to Albert's job, we notice everyone looking at us strangely; as we went to the back and found him on the floor. Still not knowing, we watched as the medics tried to resuscitate him. They got a pulse and stated they would take him to the nearest hospital. My children and I got into my car and left for the hospital. Still not knowing, I went to the receptionist desk to inquire about Albert. They informed me that he had not been admitted but they would let me know when more information become available.

As I began to pace the floor, I started calling family members to inform them of the incident. By the time they got to the hospital, the doctor sent the nurse to bring the family back. Still not knowing what was going on, I went back to Al's bed expecting to hear that he was going to be alright. The doctor with piercing eyes ask me if Al was sick and as I started to tell him of my husband complaints, he ask me if he had heart disease. I told him no, not to my knowledge. He has always been healthy. The doctors told me the symptoms that are usually associated with heart disease. I looked at the doctor and said surprisingly; "I'm the one that was diagnosed with heart disease."

A Widow's Touch

It's still not registering.

The doctor stated that they were able to resuscitate him three times and could not hold him. Still not registering, he then stated that the coroner would like to do an autopsy when someone dies at a young age from heart disease. That's when it clicked, I turned and looked at the doctors and asked, "Are you saying that my husband is dead?" I flipped! I hit the floor and commenced to kick and scream, pleading – "No Jesus No!" The nurses tried to pick me up but I wouldn't let them. I screamed this can't be true. He was here one moment and gone the next. My world was shaken upside down and nothing seemed real. I felt like I was having a bad dream and couldn't wake up. It felt as though my heart had been dropped and shattered into pieces. I can honestly say that I have had the experienced of a broken heart. I had no desire to eat or live. I began to wonder who would care for me and what will happen to our family?

I went into denial.

It was hard for me to admit or acknowledge that Albert had died. I never imagined him not being here with us. Although I had children, I was ready to go and lay right next to him. You see, Al was never sick other than a common cold, some indigestion and complaints of shoulder and arm pain with numbness. He saw the doctors for the arm and shoulder pain and was being treated through the pain clinic. He also saw the doctor for the indigestion and they diagnosed him with acid reflux. Non-the-less, because he never had high blood pressure

and had a physical every year, we never associated the above symptom with heart disease. His last physical was June 2005. He received a letter informing him that his cholesterol was high. After following up with the doctor, he informed my husband that his cholesterol was not high enough to be put on medication and he advised him to follow up in six months. Three months later, he died from a 90% blockage in two of his arteries. After finding this out, it left me bitter and angry. After anger set in, I look for someone to blame. I looked at the doctors because I felt as though they misdiagnosed him. How could it go un-detective? I looked at myself because I should have recognized the symptoms. So, guilt set in. I should have made him go to the doctor and went with him to ensure that he followed through. There was a time I felt a sense of hopelessness, pain and sorrow. Albert kept the yard up and any maintenance that was needed in the house. Whenever the lights bulbs needed replacing on my car, the oil needed changing or car needed washing, my husband handled all of these manly duties. A month after my husband transitioned, I was stopped by the police and ticketed because one head light was out. Then, someone broke in my house during daylight hours, and the next day my car was stolen from the driveway. My daughter and I felt violated and unsafe. Al loved to grill and thought he was a master chef! I enjoyed every moment of it, and took pleasure in stroking his ego. The holidays are not the same without him, and I truly miss him during those times.

The night became long.

I was lonely because I missed Albert, so much. I missed hearing his voice, hearing him sing to me, the touch of his hand, his witty ways, and our long conversations. Sometime he would talk so much, I would say under my breath I wish he would stop talking. I would love to hear his voice right now. That is a hurting and painful feeling to go through, knowing you will never hear or see your love one on this side of life, again.

Eventually, you'll realize that there is still in you, life and a lot of love to give, but the one you choose to share it with is no longer here. You ache in your heart and spirit. I believe there is a thin line between grieving and depression.

Because my heart had been shattered into pieces, at times, I did not know how to smile. There was no light in my eyes. I felt lifeless, as though I was living to die. There is a saying of feeling unbalanced, as though you are wearing one shoe. I now know what it feels like when they say a part of you is missing.

I never cared for camping.

Albert was all I knew in my life - no Brenda, no Albert, and no Albert, no Brenda. Mostly when you saw one the other was not far behind. He was so wrapped into Boy Scouting the last few years of our marriage, which cause him to do a lot of camping and to be away from home. So, Al thought why not recruit Brenda into becoming a leader, just because he wanted me there with him. Of course, I did not care for camping, but I took the training because I wanted to be with him, as well.

We had so many plans once the children graduated from high school. We were going to enjoy our lives as a couple without a care in the world, buy a RV and just travel. Getting away to places where no one could find us. I know it sounds like a fairy tale, but that's the way we thought. Unless you have lost a spouse, your first and only true love, you can't begin to understand. I believe such grief can impact you to the point of affecting your health. Eleven months after Albert died I had to have a defibrillator implant because my heart was weak. My heart stopped hours after the implant. Forcing the defibrillate to shock and restart my heart to start beating again.

Please understand I was already being treated for congestive heart failure and on heart medications, but I truly believed the grieving and the longing for my husband cause my heart to become weaker. I was under so much stress that I found myself forgetting things, my hair fell out and I lost so much weight. The ticket I got for the one head light, I was planning to go to court and state my case, but I forgot the date and had to pay an additional fine. Months later I received another ticket, forgot to go to court and was charged another fine on top of the ticket. But this time I spoke to my doctor and he wrote a letter which I used to get excused by the judge. So, you see, grief can affect your life in so many ways.

I struggled with sleeping at night because I missed Albert lying next to me.

Unexpressed grief can cause emotional and physical illnesses. Often, I would cry out to God at night when I couldn't sleep. There were days when it was hard to control my crying. I did not want anyone to see me crying, so I would go and find a quiet place or close the door to my office where no one could hear or see me. God reminded me that Jesus wept when Lazarus died and that it was okay because He understood my pain. Jesus was a man of sorrow and is very acquainted with grief. There were times when I would try to imagine what it would be like not having Albert in my life, a year or even five years from the date of his transition.

It became so overwhelming and unbearable to think clear or remember anything. God assured me I would make it; if I would just trust Him and to take one day at a time, for tomorrow would take care of itself. Just getting through today is enough. He is with me every step of the way. He would never leave me nor forsake me. God reminded me that He was there on my husband's job when we arrived, He was there in the hospital when I fell to the floor, and He was there when I could not plan the home going services. I had strong supporters in my life and God made sure they were in place. He knew I could not do this without them. I had my mother, my sisters, sister-in-law, friends and church family.

I had strong prayer warriors.

My sisters Loretta and Jennifer, who are both strong prayer warriors; were there for me. They came immediately to my side and did not leave me through the entire planning of my husband's funeral. I told them what I wanted and they planned it. They prayed with me, encouraged me, held me, cried with me, and laughed with me. They were my armor barriers keeping all negative and platitude statements from me. They were there, making sure I was not making drastic decisions and making sure no one was taking advantage of me. There were also my quiet sisters who were great listeners and strong supporters who assisted me in situations like running errands, helping with the yard and the two youngest children that were still in school.

Please understand there are seven of us and we will drop whatever we are doing to come see about each other. Nonetheless, they had to go back to their respective homes and families and resume their daily life.

Worrying about what people will say.

Crying almost every night, I felt lost and alone, too proud to call anyone. Worrying about what people would say and what they would think. The nights were long and I was unable to sleep. So, I begin to read "His Word" while crying out to God. He was there when my sisters and everyone else had to go back to their own home. He was there when I felt alone and confused, when I entered this new chapter of my life. I began to thank God for being in my life and helping get through this devastating ordeal.

He knew what I needed and when I needed things. There were times when I would cry so hard I could not see and then calmness would come over me. As I read His words, God began to show me all He had to say about the widow and the fatherless. How He would protect their property, be a Father to the fatherless, I realized I don't have to face anything without calling on Him.

Look to God for assurance.

Through all the grieving, I forgot my children would not be with me in the next two years, so just as I began to look to God for assurance and peace in my life, my last two children graduated and went off to college; opening another new chapter in my life. I was not prepared to face life without Albert in an empty nest. But God brought me through that, too. I felt nothing could be worse than what I had already gone through. That is until four years later.

My employers eliminate my job.

How many of you know that God had a plan for me and my employers had nothing to do with me being laid off. With my husband gone, I had to learn to trust God totally. It drew me closer to God and it allowed me to seek and trust Him for directions in my life. If I took my eyes off God and looked at my situation it would frighten me, but because I knew that God knew my circumstance, I had to remind myself time and time again, His plans for me was to prosper and not to harm me (Jeremiah 29:11).

The promises of God are what gave me the strength and the courage to face each day. He knew before I got to this point in my life and He also knows what the outcome will be. God reminded me of the widow in II King that loss her husband; leaving her without adequate provision. She had two sons and during that time if you owed the creditors they could take your sons and place them into slavery. Because God has a concern for widows, He became her provider and miraculously God displayed an abundant supply of the only thing she had in her house, oil. She was able to sell the oil and provide for her family. She paid off her creditors and protected her sons. God has blessed me with a talent to do the same. He has spoken to my heart and told me to trust Him. He will provide for my every need. God has blessed me with an opportunity to move on and to live a stress free and healthy life. He reminded me of my skills and talent and that there is no reason for me to worry about my finances, to be hungry, homeless or naked.

For it is said in: Matthew 6:26-30;

26 Behold the fowls of the air for they sow not, neither do they reap, nor gather into barns; yet your heavenly Father feedeth them. Are ye not much better than they?

A Widow's Touch

27 Which of you by taking thought can add one cubit unto his stature?

28 And why take ye thought for raiment? Consider the lilies of the field, how they grow; they toil not, neither do they spin:

29 And yet I say unto you, that even Solomon in all his glory was not arrayed like one of these.

30 Wherefore, if God clothe the grass of the field, which today is, and tomorrow is cast into the oven, shall he not much more clothe you, O ye of little faith?

God is good, just and faithful. Just as He promises to never leave me nor forsake me, He placed wonderful people in my life. I found myself with The Next Chapter Widows' Ministry. It is a wonderful organization where I found healing through sharing, crying, and laughter. I found healing through helping other widows by way of encouragement and being a good listener.

When I met Mary, I was having one of my crying moments and she passed me a card which introduced me to The Next Chapter Widows' Ministry, I looked at the card and of course said to myself I'm not calling her, I'm not doing this, I don't want to go into the next chapter of my life. It took about six months before I called her, but this is one of the smartest moves I ever made.

The journey I have had to walk was not easy and surely, it's not one I would want to endure or see anyone go through, but it is something many of us will face.

It is and has been wonderful to have been a part of an organization such as this. I thank God for placing Mary in the right place at the right time. I thank God for Sheila, and all the widows that I have come to know and love, in my life. Restoration has finally come!!! My heavenly Father is a heart restorer. Although this journey was hard, it was designed just for me to trust God and it taught me how to lean on Him through the toughest storms.

Grieving was like being blindfolded, even though I couldn't see for the tears that came often, nonetheless God brought me through! He carried me through this new chapter in my life and now I can smile again, I can love again, and I can now live again. In closing, I wrote this poem "Because of Christ" because I give Him the glory.

Because of Christ

Because of Christ I can face today

Because of Christ I can face tomorrow

For He knows all of my pain and He knows all of my stain

Yet He loves me just the same

In spite of my stain and through my broken heartedness

Because of Christ I can face today

Because of Christ I can face tomorrow

He sees my tears and He knows my fears

He hears my cry and knows I try

Because of His faithfulness

He was there to remove my fears and dry my eyes

He said trust me my child and live one day at a time

Because He has restored my heart and restored my joy

I can love again with a free heart

For I found myself and I found my worth

And it's because of Christ

I know we must move on with our lives, but know this; death is not the end, for one day we will reunite with our love ones. So, for now I choose to live for Christ who is the source of my life and now I wear a Garment of Praise!

Better is the end of a thing than the beginning thereof. - Ecclesiastic 7:8

Accepted Wisdom

Beliefs and Thoughts from Widows

"Don't expect everyone to understand your journey, especially if they've never had to walk your path!" - Unknown

"You never know how strong you are until being strong is the only option you have." - Unknown

"I would suggest to the widowed to do things the husband used to do, so he seems to be there with you. You will feel like you are going to make it. It's a wonderful feeling."
- Joyce Carol Oates

"And she did what she could, and that was enough..." - Unknown

"Have a good cry. Know what's on your heart? If you keep it all in, it'll tear you apart." - Unknown

"I can still feel the beat and music of your soul in my heart."
- Shannon Brooks

"Oh, I miss him so much!" - Unknown

"Sometimes, I just don't want to be alone, especially at night."
- Unknown

"It's hard seeing couples together. It reminds me of when my husband and I used to spend time with each other." - Unknown

"It's been over a year, and people expect that I should just be over him, but I still have moments when I cry." - Unknown

"I wonder sometimes if I will ever feel good on the inside again." - Unknown

"In the first year of my grief, there were times when I felt like hiding my personal story of loss and other times when I wanted to wear a sign on my body: 'be nice to me, I'm grieving,' or 'don't tic me off; I already have the world on my shoulders', or maybe even 'beware-don't upset the widow!' I need a variety of signs that I could switch out depending on my daily mood." - Elizabeth Berriem

Mary's Closing Message

Over the past twenty-five years, I have learned to put my faith in God. In spite of the loss of my husband, Al. God has shown me that He will always be a comforter and a provider for me and my children. Sometimes, the road seems very dark and lonely, but I encourage you to keep your focus on God and He will get you through—day by day. There is no secret to what God can do. What He has done for me, He will certainly do for you. I can now look back and see how God had prepared me for this next chapter of my life.

Be encouraged!

Mary M. Hollis, Director
The Next Chapter Widows' Ministry

About The Next Chapter Widows' Ministry — Our Purpose

To exemplify love to widows through regular encouragement and information about the many decisions to be made in the first three years after the loss of a spouse.

Sheila A. Coley
President

Mary M. Hollis
Director

The Next Chapter Widows' Ministry was created to help women recover from the loss of the most significant person in their lives—their husbands. Widows have no specific identity. They may be young or old, poor or wealthy, with or without children. The loss could have been expected or sudden. While there are many diverse situations, the common link is the marital relationship that was created, regardless of the years.

The emotional distress of becoming a widow can be overwhelming. When someone you have shared secrets with, made love with, laughed with, been angry with, and a host of other scenarios dies, that person is missed. No one can fill that emptiness. Widows have immediate questions that must be answered;

"Who really understands what I am going through?"

A Widow's Touch

"Who can I talk to when I need, someone to care about me?"

"Who can help me with all the details?"

"How do I cope with these new life decisions?"

These questions and challenges gave birth to our widow's ministry. If—it's time to turn to the next chapter in your life, we are here to help you. God is the giver of life. He is also the one who takes it away. With the spiritual insight and personal experience of our facilitators, feel assured that you are not alone.

"The Next Chapter Widows' Ministry" shows you love through regular encouragement and information about the many decisions you may encounter in the first three years after the loss of your spouse. We will welcome you, when you are ready. Call (980) 494-3697 (980-4WIDOWS) to receive a warm welcome and to get additional information.

Spiritual and Inspirational Internet Radio Show:
To be uplifted, tune in on Tuesdays at 10:00 P.M. (EST.)

Call (347) 850-8413 or login to:
www.blogtalkradio.com/TheNextChapter

Connect through Email: TNCwidows@gmail.com to share your personal needs and concerns as a widow or to share your thoughts on *A Widow's Touch.*

Visit our website: www.tncwidows.com

Visit us on Facebook: "Like" us and leave comments

A Widow's Touch

The Next Chapter Widows' Ministry
Recommended Spiritual Reading for Widows

Psalm 23

Psalm 27

Psalm 40

Psalm 46: 10 -11

Psalm 121

Isaiah 41:10

1 Timothy 5:3

1 Peter 5:7

Future volumes of A Widows' Touch

The stories in this first volume were submitted by a variety of widows, with hope to touch many. From the very start of this inspiring book, it has been our goal to encourage people from around the world to submit their true short stories for publication. We will welcome stories that influence, effect the emotions and stir the heart.

We are asking for well-written, personal, inspirational pieces showing how faith in God can inspire, encourage, heal, and give hope. We are looking for human-interest stories with a spiritual application, affirming ways in which Christian faith is expressed in everyday life. You can become a blessing to other widows by sharing your story about your first three years as a widow in 50-1,500 words. Your story must be told with drama, description, and dialogue.

To request submission guidelines, visit our website:

www.tncwidows.com or send your request to our Email: TNCwidows@gmail.com.

At this time, fees are not paid for printed stories. However, you will be given credit for your contribution to The Next Chapter Widows' Ministry. Proceeds received from future volumes will be used to support the Widow's Ministry.

Creating a Movement...

Take a minute and jot down your thoughts on how the stories impacted you or start noting key points about your personal experiences as a widow or a friend of a widow.

_____

_____

_____

_____

_____

_____

_____

_____

_____

_____

_____

_____

_____

_____

_____

_____

_____

_____

_____

_____

_____

_____

_____

Notes:_____

_____
_____
_____
_____
_____
_____
_____
_____
_____
_____
_____
_____
_____
_____
_____
_____
_____
_____
_____
_____
_____
_____
_____
_____
_____
_____
_____
_____

Made in the USA
Columbia, SC
24 June 2019